ACCESS TO OIL—THE UNITED STATES RELATIONSHIPS WITH SAUDI ARABIA AND IRAN

PRINTED AT THE REQUEST OF
HENRY M. JACKSON, *Chairman*
COMMITTEE ON ENERGY AND NATURAL RESOURCES
UNITED STATES SENATE

University Press of the Pacific
Honolulu, Hawaii

Access to Oil: The United States Relationships with
Saudi Arabia and Iran

Prepared by
Fern Racine Gold
Melvin A. Conant

For
Committee on Energy and Natural Resources
United States Senate

ISBN: 1-4102-0388-3

Copyright © 2003 by University Press of the Pacific

Reprinted from the 1977 edition

University Press of the Pacific
Honolulu, Hawaii
http://www.universitypressofthepacific.com

All rights reserved, including the right to reproduce
this book, or portions thereof, in any form.

MEMORANDUM OF THE CHAIRMAN

To Members of the Senate Committee on Energy and Natural Resources:

Access to energy has become an international issue of overriding importance, particularly since the Arab embargo 4 years ago. The complex interrelationship of political, military and economic factors governing such access was analyzed in the pioneering study of the "Geopolitics of Energy" published by the Committee earlier this year.

For the United States, access to secure supplies of foreign oil has become an increasingly vital policy goal with the decline of domestic production and our growing dependence on oil imports. Saudi Arabia and Iran represent a significant source of oil for the United States and a crucial source for Western Europe and Japan. This study attempts to evaluate the relationships between the United States and Saudi Arabia and the United States and Iran in terms of their contribution to access to oil.

The significance of these relationships cannot be emphasized too strongly. A decade from now, the entire industrial world will be competing for available Middle East supply on an unprecedented scale. The U.S. relationships with Saudi Arabia and Iran may well be the critical key for supply security from this region, not only for the United States but for other industrial nations as well.

Given this prospect, a full understanding of the nature and significance of these vital relationships seems essential. While the continuation of the relationships depends primarily on the political acceptance by Saudi Arabia and Iran of the arrangements involved, there is much we can do to increase the prospects for such acceptance in the years ahead.

This study was prepared for the Committee by Fern Racine Gold and Melvin A. Conant, who also collaborated on the "Geopolitics of Energy." The Committee is grateful for their contribution to our work on international energy issues. Because of the study's significance for energy policy, I have asked that it be published as a Committee print for the use of Members of Congress and others involved in the development of energy policy.

HENRY M. JACKSON, *Chairman.*

ACCESS TO OIL—THE UNITED STATES RELATIONSHIPS WITH SAUDI ARABIA AND IRAN

Prepared by

FERN RACINE GOLD

and

MELVIN A. CONANT

at the request of

HENRY M. JACKSON, *Chairman*
Committee on Energy and Natural Resources
United States Senate

CONTENTS

	Page
Memorandum of the Chairman	III
Summary	IX

Part I

I. Access to oil	3
Introduction	3
Access under the colonial system	3
Access and the period of commercial dominance	4
Changes in the international environment	5
Nuclear stalemate	5
Post-war recovery	5
Independence and nationalism	6
The geopolitics of oil	6
The United States and access to oil	8
II. Special relationships	11
Questions to be addressed	12
Strategy	12

Part II.—The Franco-Algerian Example, 1962–73

I. Special relationship by design	17
Introduction	17
Historical development	17
The Evian Declarations	19
Oil	20
The 1965 oil agreement	20
Revision of the 1965 agreement	21
Postnationalization developments	23
Algeria	25
France	27
Conclusion	28

Part III.—Saudi Arabia

I. Historical developments	35
Introduction	35
The House of Saud	35
Society	37
Oil, World War II, and relations with the West	38
II. Economic developments	41
Introduction	41
Domestic economic development plans and goals	42
Prospects	44
Foreign investment	46
Foreign aid	48
Military purchases	49
Implications	50
III. Political developments	53
Introduction	53
The political system	53
The Royal Family	54
Political developments	56
Implications	57

	Page
IV. International relations	59
Introduction	59
Policy objectives and the Arab-Israeli conflict	59
Radical regimes	60
The Organization of Petroleum Exporting Countries	61
General international affairs	62
Implications	63

Part IV.—Iran

	Page
I. Historical relations with the West	67
Introduction	67
Britain and Russia	67
The United States	71
II. Current foreign relations: The Iranian and United States perspective	75
Introduction	75
Soviet Union	75
The United States	76
Western Europe and Japan	77
The Gulf	78
Elsewhere	80
Nuclear option	82
Military purchases	82
Implications—The U.S. perspective	83
III. Economic developments	85
Introduction	85
Structure of the economy and development goals	85
The nature of the task	87
Political uses of economic development	90
Land reform	90
Profit sharing and share participation	91
The White Revolution	92
Private investors	92
The Fifth Plan and beyond	93
Implications	96
Oil policy	96
Other implications	97
IV. The political system	99
Introduction	99
Political development	99
The Shah and the Monarchy	101
Goals	103
Functioning of the system	104
Political and social forces	104
Political dynamics	106
Alternative regimes and implications	107

Part V

	Page
I. Implications for the United States	111

SUMMARY

When in 1973 the oil producing countries assumed control of oil prices and production levels, they served notice that the traditional means whereby the industrialized countries secured access to oil would no longer suffice. Access to foreign oil supplies would no longer be determined by the commercial interests of the private international oil companies in supplying, more or less automatically, the needs of the industrialized countries. Nor would the familiar system of concessions by which companies had obtained paramount control over the disposition of oil—and the rate of production—continue to function as before.

At the same time, some degree of assurance of access to foreign supplies of oil is essential; in particular, the economic, political and military well-being of the industrialized countries depends on their having access to adequate and continuous supplies of oil. Moreover, in spite of domestic energy efforts—which are lagging in any event—the dependence of the industrialized countries on oil as the principal energy source and, therefore, on oil imports will continue well into the 1990's. The question of access to oil will thus occupy the highest levels of government for a very considerable period of time.

It is not that the needs of the industrialized world will be neglected by exporters—most of whom depend upon access to the industrial markets. It is rather that those needs now join a host of factors—political and economic—which will determine the volumes and terms of oil available for world trade. The calculations will now be made by a small group of oil exporters whose interests and political objectives may not coincide with those of the industrialized countries.

In effect, 1973 represented a culmination of interrelated trends in international relations which had been developing since World War II—decolonization, the growing reluctance to use military force, rapid economic recovery and growth in Europe and Japan. It is against this background, and the continuing need for oil imports by the industrialized countries, that new mechanisms of access to secure and adequate oil supplies will have to evolve.

Any consideration of developing mechanisms of access must include an analysis of the United States, Saudi Arabia, and Iran and the relations among and between them. These three actors and their interaction will be important determinants of adequate and continuous oil supplies in world trade. The creation of close bilateral relations between countries is one mechanism by which future access to raw materials might be obtained. This report marks an effort to evaluate the relationships between the United States and Iran and the United States and Saudi Arabia in terms of their contribution to access to oil.

The French attempted to create a relationship with Algeria with particular regard for an assured supply of oil. It is an important and instructive example of one mechanism by which a developed country attempted to secure access to the natural resources of a developing country through close and multiple bilateral ties. The report, therefore, includes a section on the history and results of that undertaking. Especially interesting is the conclusion that when the mutuality of interests are solid and enduring, a "special relationship" may not be necessary, in fact it may serve to involve political aspects which eventually become counterproductive.

Saudi Arabia will be increasingly the major source of incremental oil supplies. Saudi decisions on production levels could spell the difference between adequate supplies and absolute shortage. At the same time, to the extent that Saudi Arabia is willing to continue to produce at levels adequate to meet world oil import demand, it will accumulate financial resources which can not be effectively utilized domestically. On the basis of Saudi national interests, narrowly defined, it may not be in the Saudi interest to produce at increasing rates to meet world oil demand while accumulating revenue in excess of its capacity to utilize it. There is considerable debate within the kingdom on this point and Saudi domestic economic, social and political developments are, therefore, important determinants of access to oil in world trade.

Iran is the second largest OPEC producer. It has also assumed the role of protector of the conservative tradition in the Gulf, guarantor of the oil sea-lanes and it has set about creating the military capability for these roles. Internal Iranian economic and political developments, as well as the external objectives of the regime, are also of concern as they may affect the continuous flow of oil.

The United States, for different reasons and at different times, has created a relationship between itself and Iran, then with Saudi Arabia, which has acquired exceptional importance to oil importing nations as the only available means for helping assure security and continuity of oil, at needed volumes. Thus the most vital oil interests of Europe and Japan are seen to depend upon commitments assumed to have been made involving military undertakings and economic considerations including—at least in the case of Saudi Arabia—some understanding regarding the level of production and price.

But it is not Europe and Japan alone which will be affected by conditions in the Gulf. The issue of dependable supply for the United States arises out of the U.S. energy posture—one in which the need for overseas sources of oil supply will be of continuing, vital importance. Forecasts of import dependence for the United States and the industrial world generally agree on this point. Additionally, the United States is constrained in its freedom to act internationally if the move risks the continuous flow of imported oil. The Soviet Union presently has no such constraint.

Moreover, forecasts emphasize that for the next decade and more there is no realistic prospect of sufficient additional reserves being discovered, developed and brought to market to diminish the peculiar significance of Middle East reserves to the consuming world.

In short, by the late eighties, the industrial world—including eventually the U.S.S.R.—will be competing on an unprecedented scale for available Middle East supply.

In this setting, the United States, by virtue of its commercial oil interests' long-standing monopoly over the disposition of Saudi crude, now reinforced by the 1974 conclusion of a "special relationship" embracing economic and military agreements, is very widely regarded among its allies and by Arabs and Iranians as having secured preferential and near-exclusive access to Saudi oil. Given the extraordinary importance of Saudi oil production to the world generally, the U.S. relationship is considered key to supply security.

A somewhat comparable stake exists with Iran—the second largest exporter of oil. The U.S. relationship with Iran began in World War II, became involved in oil in the fifties and has continued, along with the U.S. military stake in the defense of the region, to be "special" in every sense while not involving such direct dependence on Iranian oil as in the case of Saudi Arabia.

It is these two sets of relationships in the context of the internal and external factors in Iran and Saudi Arabia which is the focus of this report. In reviewing these Iranian and Saudi considerations, the attempt is made to view them from the perspectives of their historical experiences as well as of their contemporary scene. How they may perceive their relationships with the United States is of exceptional importance.

Interests which lie outside a "special relationship" or preferential access to someone's oil may be of greatest consequence. For example, while it is the United States which has a link to Iran and one to Saudi Arabia which no other country can forge, the importance of Iranian oil to U.S. imports is negligible— some 6 percent—and the importance of Saudi oil to U.S. imports is some 22 percent with the bulk of oil from both countries going very largely to Europe and Japan. This anomaly in special relationships, where the benefit is usually direct to each party, adds a new dimension to the U.S. link to each producer. One can argue that while the oil benefit is nowhere near so great to the United States as it is to European and Japanese importers for which it is vital, the U.S. relationship with Iran and Saudi Arabia serves the collective security interests of its allies in helping assure a continuous and adequate flow of oil—if not yet at a price which is within their capacity to pay.

This appreciation of the oil security role of the United States is not, however, unqualified. While the present U.S. dependence upon Saudi oil is far less consequential than Europe's or Japan's, neither of the latter ignore the possible implications to their supply of the apparent decision of Saudi Arabia to make available to the American oil companies involved in ARAMCO—which developed the oil resources of the kingdom—as much as 7 million barrels of oil each day—nearly 70 percent of current Saudi productive capacity and over four times the volume of Saudi crude imported today into the United States. Will this supply be "reserved" for U.S. needs? Will the U.S. Government come to affect the destination of these 7 million barrels per day, exercising its influence through the American oil companies? Or will the companies be able to continue to supply unhampered by considerations other than the meeting of their contractual commitments?

These aspects may seem of sufficient consequences but there are other factors included in this report which are not normally considered in evaluations of the relationships. There is a very long historical background to the role which Iran intends to perform to which it wishes the United States to conform, and unless the origins of it are understood one cannot comprehend the contemporary scene including the link to the United States.

The report stresses the great importance to Iran's national memory of a succession of British and Russian efforts either to capture much of Iran or negate the influence of the other over a particular regime. The search for a third party—in this case the United States—to balance off or divide the others has much to say about the Iranian perspective of the relationship with the United States.

Similarly, the desire of Ibn Saud to limit the expansion of British influence in the Gulf and in the Arabian Peninsula, and his choice of American oil companies to make the point—presuming upon U.S. Government backing of the companies—to keep the British at a distance, influenced his heirs in perpetuating a favored relationship with the United States.

The United States has interests in common with those of Iran and Saudi Arabia however complicated the relationships may become as different strains upon these Middle East kingdoms, arising principally out of internal problems, may pit the oil power of Arabia against the ambitions of the Shah. Still, the common interests are real and of great importance to both; (a) protection of the oilfields and related facilities; (b) containment of the Soviet Union's efforts to extend Soviet influence in the region; and (c) support of nonradical regimes in the Middle East. And one could probably add: (d) earliest possible resolution of the Arab-Israeli dispute as a major issue hindering the achievement of objectives (b) and (c).

Which is not to infer that the interests of Iran and of Saudi Arabia are alike; they are not. As is brought out in this report while their political and economic goals are generally the same, there are worlds of difference between them when one considers size of population, compares the scale of the industrialization process, the extent to which different stages of social change affect their undertakings, and the extraordinary dependence upon oil revenue in the case of Iran and the need for much less oil revenue in the instance of Saudi Arabia. As is also brought out in this report, the Israeli issue has greatly complicated the U.S. relationship with Saudi Arabia and threatens to affect the price and volume of oil from the kingdom.

In short, the stress in this report is on a process of profound change occurring in both countries rather than stability. One can speculate endlessly about the rate and sweep of this change but the emphasis is correct. The United States is attempting to assure the continuous and adequate flow of oil from a region of increasing complexity and undergoing rapid rates of change.

The principal conclusions of this report are—

(1) The U.S. security interest in the Gulf is of exceptional importance to nations importing significant volumes from the region—and to the producing nations themselves.

(2) That security interest may yet prove to be the most effective inducement to the Saudis to produce at a rate which is considerably above the level actually required to generate revenue to meet Saudi internal and external objectives.

(3) The U.S. connection with Saudi Arabia, and the one with Iran has put the United States into a special position in Gulf affairs. It was not planned but it is a fact of great significance. As the internal strains

within each country multiply, as we expect, these will generate further tensions within the Gulf; the U.S. role in future developments will be even more complicated.

(4) Finally, the meaning and durability of the U.S. relationships with Iran and Saudi Arabia depend very largely on the continuing political acceptance by either kingdom of the arrangements. Unless this political factor remains secure, and the undertakings of the parties remain harmonious and to their mutual benefit, everything will fall apart in the Gulf.

(5) Yet the prospect is one of change, of instability in a region of utmost consequence to the industrial, oil importing world. In this respect, while the security interest of the United States has been emphasized, the ultimate determinant of the Gulf's future may well be the success or failure of the producer nations' intensive efforts in economic development. The U.S. role in these efforts, already considerable, needs to be given particular attention so that to the extent that it is within our means to help assure success, we spare no effort to assist.

MELVIN A. CONANT,
Project Director.

PART I

I. ACCESS TO OIL

INTRODUCTION

In 1973, the oil exporting countries asserted their ability to unilaterally set oil prices and production levels. That act served notice that the previous means by which the industrialized countries secured access to oil through the major international oil companies acting in accordance with their commercial interests in supplying, more or less automatically, the needs of the developed countries would no longer suffice to determine the total amount of available oil supplies, the worldwide allocation of those supplies, and the terms on which supplies were made available.

Yet access to oil and security of supply are vital to the industrialized countries for whom there is no immediately available alternative to oil and oil imports as an energy source. If access will no longer be determined by the sheer needs of the industrialized countries, how will access be determined, via what mechanisms and on what terms? Against the background of changing international relationships, what alternative means of access exist or might be created; that is, international commodity agreements, consumer organizations, producer organizations, producer-consumer organizations, bilateral arrangements, etc.? Are they mutually exclusive or might/should several mechanisms coexist? Do they contribute to security of supply and/or other international objectives? At what cost, to whom?

The central concern of this study is an evaluation of the relationships between the United States and Saudi Arabia and the United States and Iran in terms of their contribution to securing access to oil.

ACCESS UNDER THE COLONIAL SYSTEM

The very need to phrase the issue of access to energy in the form of questions is a reflection of the changes which have been evolving in international economic and political relations since World War II. In preceding periods, if access was in question at all, it involved rivalries among the great powers and would have been resolved by them alone.

The colonial system provided an essentially automatic mechanism by which the metropolitan countries acquired access to raw materials. This is not to suggest that the impetus for colonial expansion can be explained by economic causes alone, or even predominantly. Strong political, strategic, prestige and humanitarian factors coincided or reinforced the desire to preempt raw materials to bolster one's own power and to deny similar advantages to others and the motivations in each particular case were probably some mix of all of these.

For our purposes however, the central point is that the structure and norms of international relations under the colonial system, made it inconceivable that a colony could withhold raw materials from the metropolitan country or demand better terms with impunity. Colonialism as a system of international relations depended on the ability and the willingness of the metropolitan country to enforce its dominance, even at the expense of a quite legitimate recourse to military force, and the weakness and inability of the colonies to oppose it.

ACCESS AND THE PERIOD OF COMMERCIAL DOMINANCE

The period during which commercial organizations and considerations dominated the mechanisms of access to raw materials actually overlapped the period of colonialism, but also survived its decline—not however, untainted by the association. The metropolitan countries, having established their political control over the colonies, often left the economic sphere to their private companies.

This was certainly the case with regard to oil. British interest in Persia and the Gulf initially reflected British concern to protect the communications lines and the territorial integrity of its Indian empire from Russian encroachments. Only later, with the conversion of the Royal Navy to oil fuel just prior to World War I, did the interest in oil per se add another dimension to British interest in Persia. The development of Persian oil was left to the Anglo-Persian Oil Co. (now British Petroleum) in which, however, the British Government did purchase a majority share in 1914.

Following World War I and with the dawning recognition of the future importance of oil, France successfully compelled the British, as part of the war settlement, to give it a share in the Turkish Petroleum Co. (later the Iraq Petroleum Co., IPC) in 1920.

The American Government, convinced of an impending oil shortage at home, was eager to end British and French monopolization of Middle East oil. The Government succeeded through diplomatic initiatives in obtaining the participation of American private companies in the IPC concession in 1928, as it did for the Gulf Oil Co. in Kuwait, the Standard Oil Co. of California (SOCAL) in Bahrain and a group of American companies in Iran. Only in the case of Saudi Arabia was the concession awarded on the basis of more nearly commercial considerations, without U.S. Government diplomatic intervention.

Once the respective governments had secured a place for "their" oil companies in the Middle East concessions, they retired and trusted in the companies' commercial interests to provide adequate oil supplies to the domestic market. The vindication of that trust came with the phenomenal increase in the use of oil as an energy source after World War II, an increase made possible by the very considerable managerial, technical, and capital assets which the companies possessed and which they applied in a highly efficient manner.

In spite of continuing challenges to the role of the international oil companies and the concession system from the oil producing countries and government/national and "independent" oil companies, it is only realistic to note that until 1973, consuming countries could still rely on the commercial operations of these firms to provide adequate oil supplies.

But the system depended first on the colonial pattern of relationships and after colonialism's decline, the functioning of the commercial mechanism depended on a particular structure of international relations—a structure created and dominated by the West and Japan and which continued past the end of empire.

CHANGES IN THE INTERNATIONAL ENVIRONMENT

Post-war developments in international politics undermined the international oil system and set the stage for 1973 oil developments. Three quite different but related factors deserve emphasis here.

NUCLEAR STALEMATE

With the advent of a nuclear weapons capability in the U.S.S.R. in 1949, the use of military force became an increasingly less palatable alternative given the risk of superpower confrontation and the possibility of escalation. Military power still distinguished among states but with its associated higher risks it became a last resort, to be used only for the most serious of challenges to the most vital national interests of nations and only where the proxy means of competition failed.

Moreover, with increasing numbers of states in the international system having little realistic prospect of being able to marshal military force or to oppose it, and with the memory of World War II still fresh, the norms of the international system increasingly came to regard the use of military force as illegitimate.

A most critical development which served to transform the international oil relationships with producers was the shattering retreat of British and French forces from Egypt and the Suez in 1956, with the United States standing back from a military rescue and, indeed, calling upon these hitherto "great powers" to cease and desist. Suez marked the end; the former imperial powers could not impose their views by military means.

The declining legitimacy associated with military force and the increasing inability and unwillingness to utilize it had two major effects. In the first instance, the effect was a leveling one and if force was not to be used, even the smallest state could challenge a superpower with relative impunity. Second, the definition of what constituted power (the ability to influence others), was altered; if power was conferred less by the possession of a military establishment, other elements, including perhaps, control of a vital natural resource, had to be included in the calculation of relative power.

POSTWAR RECOVERY

The post-war world witnessed the rapid reconstruction and recovery in the industrialized countries in Europe and Japan. Bolstered by American aid and a network of new institutions established in the aftermath of World War II, economic recovery and rapid economic growth were reflected in the equally rapid growth in demand for raw materials and particularly, cheap oil.

Japan was almost totally dependent on imported sources of raw materials and practically 100 percent dependent on foreign sources of oil. Europe, while less dependent than Japan, still required large imports of raw materials, including oil supplies. The decade of the 1960's witnessed the rapid conversion of the industrialized economies from coal to oil and by the 1970's even the United States, with a far more generous resource endowment than either Europe or Japan, came increasingly to depend on foreign sources for a growing portion of its oil supplies.

INDEPENDENCE AND NATIONALISM

The third characteristic of the postwar world which changed the structure of international relations was the growing sense of nationalism in the remnants of empire. By the early 1960's, 800 million people in more than 60 states achieved independence.

The international system, in terms of sheer numbers, was no longer dominated by the West (including Japan), but by an increasingly vocal group of less developed countries. For these countries, colonialism had not ended with the attainment of political independence; it had merely assumed a different form as economic control now substituted for political domination.

The post-war economic institutions, in the view of these countries, also suited the interests of the developed countries and increasingly they saw in the international economic and political systems, a structure of relations which not only did not serve their interests but was actually inimical to them.

The economic growth of the industrialized countries was seen by these newly independent countries to be dependent on LDC raw materials, exploited by the giant multinational corporations in the companies' interests and in the interests of the developed countries but with minimal and residual benefit to the less developed countries wherein the resources were located. Control over their natural resources was then a necessary prerequisite to increasing their share of the benefits to be derived from natural resource exploitation. Control of their natural resources, often their one and only natural resource, was vital to that economic growth and development which alone could give real meaning to the political independence already achieved.

It was the interaction of these three changes in postwar international relations which provided the permissive setting for 1973 oil developments. The increasing ambivalence regarding the use of military force and the rapidly increasing demand for oil imports shifted the balance of power in favor of those countries where the resources were located. The oil producing countries, united in the Organization of Petroleum Exporting Countries (OPEC), seized the opportunity for full control of their oil resources, introducing new factors in the question of access to oil.

THE GEOPOLITICS OF OIL

Access to oil is essential to the developed countries and will continue to be so for as long as oil is the primary energy source for these countries.

The geopolitical significance of oil lies in two propositions: (1) Oil, as fuel and feedstock, is a vital necessity for the continued economic, political and military well-being of the industrialized countries; and, (2) oil is located in, and controlled by, a small group of less developed countries whose interests may overlap those of the developed countries, but are not necessarily identical to them.

In spite of post-1973 efforts by the industrialized countries to reduce their dependence on oil, it is now generally agreed that oil will continue to provide about one half of the free world's energy supply through 1985 and probably into the 1990's. Even if conservation efforts and the development of alternative and indigenous energy sources should reduce oil's share in total energy supply, the volumetric demands for oil will continue to increase. In 1985, oil may represent 70 percent of Japan's primary energy supply, 50 percent of Western Europe's energy consumption, and 40 percent of U.S. energy consumption.

Dependence on oil is tantamount to dependence on oil imports: Japan has virtually no indigenous oil supplies and will continue to import close to 100 percent of its oil requirements; European oil-import dependence in 1985 is estimated to be in the range of 70 to 85 percent even taking account of North Sea oil developments and the U.S. dependence on oil imports is forecast to be in the 50 percent range through 1985. While oil represents a smaller share of the U.S. energy budget and imports account for a smaller percentage of oil supply than is true in the cases of Europe and Japan, the entire industrialized world will remain heavily dependent on oil and oil imports.

Dependence on oil imports in turn is equal to dependence on OPEC oil. Given historical rates of discovery and the long leadtimes associated with the development of a new discovery, there is no realistic prospect that enough oil will be found or, if found, developed rapidly enough to challenge OPEC's position as the primary source of oil in world trade.

Moreover, additional oil available for world trade will increasingly originate in the countries of the Gulf, particularly Saudi Arabia, as production in other OPEC countries peaks. This means that the industrialized countries will depend more heavily on those several countries: Kuwait, the Emirates, Saudi Arabia and possibly Iraq, (1) that are already flooded with revenue (except perhaps Iraq) far beyond their capacity to effectively utilize it at home or to invest it profitably abroad; and (2) who share a common political purpose vis-a-vis the Arab-Israeli dispute and with regard to Pan-Arab sentiment.

At the same time, while it is likely that the Soviet Union will also need to import additional quantities of oil (now for its own account and not simply to maintain an effective mechanism of control over Eastern Europe), the Soviet problem is not one of resource scarcity as it may be in the United States and is in Europe (unless the more optimistic forecasts of North Sea possibilities prove out) and Japan. The Soviet Union apparently has abundant energy resources—oil, gas, coal and uranium—and it is a matter of time, priorities, technology, and the application of sufficient resources to develop them. The Soviet Union alone may have a potential for energy self-sufficiency—a point further underlining the seriousness to the industrialized countries of the question of access to oil.

Post-1973, with the greater involvement of producing governments in international oil, the prospect is one in which political factors will bear more heavily on the issue of access. The needs and concerns of the oil producing countries will be weighed more heavily than in the past in the determination of the level of oil supply in world trade and the disposition and price of that oil.

It is not so much that commercial factors no longer obtain at all in determining oil supply and its terms; the producing countries do have an economic interest in the continued flow of oil to markets which are dominated by the industrialized countries. Rather, it is that commercial interests now vie with other economic and political interests in determining the continuity and adequacy of oil flowing in world trade. And commercial interests may look considerably different when viewed from the perspective of the oil producing countries.

The calculation of terms now is being made in the producing countries and not so totally in the more familiar boardrooms of the major international oil companies. Under these circumstances, how can the consuming countries bring their interests into the calculation—their influence to bear in the determination of access and how can access to oil be made more secure?

The United States and Access to Oil

This then is the international environment in which the United States will seek access to oil. It is an environment characterized by:

(1) Rapidly changing international economic and political relationships, involving not merely oil producers and oil consumers but also relations among the countries of the Western and Japanese alliances as they compete for oil available in world trade and more general developed-developing country relations;

(2) The politicization of oil supplies as producer and consumer governments involve themselves more deeply in international oil, introducing new economic and political factors in the determination of available oil supplies and the terms on which access is secured;

(3) The inescapable dependence of the industrialized countries on oil and oil imports and the greater dependence of Europe and Japan on foreign oil sources relative to the United States;

(4) The more favorable resource endowment of the USSR vis-a-vis the Western and Japanese alliances; and

(5) The reluctance on the part of the industrialized countries (for all intents and purposes the U.S.), to resort to overt military force to secure access to oil supplies, except perhaps as a last resort.

Even if the United States is able to reduce its oil imports to the 6-million-barrels-a-day target in the President's energy plan (and it is thought unlikely) from the 10 to 12 million barrels-a-day forecast in the absence of such efforts, the United States will be involved in international oil to a substantial degree. Moreover, the continued dependence of Western Europe and Japan on oil imports and the plight of the non-oil LDC's will involve the United States in international oil.

The actions that the United States takes domestically to reduce its dependence on oil imports will be an essential factor in determining access to those supplies which remain crucial; with reduced U.S. oil-import demand, the oil supply/demand situation would less clearly favor the oil producers (in the absence of an OPEC production programing scheme) and the question of access to oil for Western Europe and Japan might be considerably eased with a reduction in U.S. import demand freeing quantities of oil for sale elsewhere. Access to those supplies still needed may be easier to the extent that the need for access is reduced by U.S. domestic energy efforts.

But 6 million barrels per day is still a substantial figure, almost equivalent to Japan's total import requirements, and the concern is to secure access to those supplies of oil which will remain essential in spite of U.S. energy efforts. In the first instance, access implies the availability of oil imports in quantities adequate to meet U.S. domestic demand. These supplies must be continuous and they must be available at prices which do as little damage to the U.S. economy as possible. These three—adequacy, continuity, and "reasonable" prices form part of the definition of access.

At the same time, U.S. interests demand that the needs of Western Europe, Japan, and the non-oil LDC's receive attention in U.S. policymaking. The United States and the alliance system could not remain untouched by the economic and political ramifications of oil supply disruptions or shortages or prices so high as to result in shortages in Western Europe and Japan.

Any temporary advantage to the United States in terms of economic growth and international competitiveness (given the smaller impact of higher oil prices on the U.S. economy relative to the impact on Western Europe and Japan) might be dissipated by: (1) lower or less rapidly increasing standards of living and political instability abroad; (2) reduced economic growth and hence reduced demand for U.S. exports; and (3) reduced European and Japanese production for export and hence the reduced capacity to finance imports in the industrialized countries which represent the United States major trading partners.

In addition, the prospects for economic growth and development in the most promising, non-oil LDC's have been severely damaged by higher energy prices and the political ramifications of this fact remain to be seen. Moreover, the inability of some nonoil LDC's and some industrialized countries to continue to finance oil imports except by recourse to international public or private borrowings, which then cannot be repaid and which are simply rolled over again and again, threatens the international banking, monetary and financial systems and, of necessity, concerns the United States.

"Access" then includes adequacy and continuity of supply at "reasonable" prices not merely for the United States but for a wider grouping of countries whose futures will affect the United States. Access comes to include a concern with the total supply of oil available for world trade and its allocation worldwide. It is these five—adequacy, continuity (security), "reasonable" prices, total supply of oil available for world trade, and the allocation of that supply—which constitute access in terms of the interests of the United States.

In the context of current and evolving international relations how might the United States act to secure access to oil? Other consuming governments have tried to secure access to raw materials by establishing strong bilateral ties with a particular producing country; the the case of France and Algeria is an outstanding example. The U.S. Government's response has included the institutionalization of "special relationships" with Saudi Arabia and Iran in partial answer to this question.

II. SPECIAL RELATIONSHIPS

These relationships, developing at least since the late thirties for Saudi Arabia and as early as the first decades of this century for Iran, have been described as mechanisms of access and means of guaranteeing greater security of supply. Moreover, it is suggested that through these relationships the considerable economic, political and military power of the United States can be brought to bear more directly in the determination of access to oil.

And yet these relationships, institutionalized in the 1974 Joint Commissions, appear to have evolved without conscious thought as to their nature; scope; mutual obligations; impact on the parties involved; and, impact on third countries. They apparently just grew. Their contributions to security of supply and access to oil have been more often assumed than the subject of critical evaluation and assessment.

The pivotal role of Saudi Arabia, with its immense oil reserves and apparently limited absorptive capacity and its position as the major source of spare producing capacity, has already been described. If access is to be determined, to a greater extent than in the past, by the needs and goals of the oil producing countries, then greater knowledge of Saudi Arabia—oil producer and exporter par excellence—and its economic, social, political and international needs and goals is critical. The importance of Iran as the second largest OPEC oil exporter and defender of the oil access routes makes similar knowledge regarding Iran essential.

The importance of the United States in terms of the sheer weight of its participation in the international oil market, its economic and political influence and as the only free world nation with the capability of militarily defending the Gulf region or intervening in the event of necessity is acknowledged. These three actors—Saudi Arabia, Iran, and the United States—and their interrelationships will thus be crucial in determining access to oil.

Under these circumstances the implications of United States-Saudi relations and United States-Iranian relations must be the subject of analysis rather than the subject of a profound wishful thinking. It may be that the relationship between the United States and each of these exporters does contribute to security of supply and access to oil, but this must be determined rather than taken for granted and it must be assessed in terms of alternative or supplementary means of access; special relationships may be only one among many means of securing access.

Moreover, to say that the relationships contribute to security of supply and access to oil, does not imply that the relationships, in their current form, are the only or best means of securing access. Rather, these statements could be more properly phrased in the form of questions.

Questions To Be Addressed

It is in these terms that the United States-Saudi, and the United States-Iranian relationships need to be assessed. The contribution of these relationships to greater security of supply and the more general question of access to oil is a subject for investigation, not an established fact. It is necessary to ask if the relationships between the United States and Saudi Arabia and the United States and Iran enhance security of supply and stability of terms?

The degree to which they do so may depend on: (1) the interests of the participants served by the relationship; (2) the saliency of those interests compared to other interests of the participants; (3) the degree to which interests are mutual rather than converging or partially overlapping; and, (4) the degree to which the United States, Saudi Arabia, or Iran see no viable alternative mechanism for protecting and promoting their individual and collective interests.

In addition, it is necessary to ask whether the existence of the relationships actually affects the behavior of the participants in the desired directions? Finally, from the perspective of each country, what mutual obligations are being exchanged and how balanced are the costs and benefits to each country? Are the perceptions of obligations undertaken by others accurate?

To the extent that the relationships contribute to more secure access to oil, it is necessary to inquire as to the factors which contribute to the durability of such relationships and the degree to which these factors can be deliberately engineered, if they do not exist naturally? Does the longevity of the relationship depend on: (1) particular regimes; that is, the continued dominance of the current branch of the Saudi Royal Family or the Shah's regime in Iran; (2) particular political systems; or, (3) particular domestic, economic and political groups?

Even if the United States-Saudi and United States-Iranian ties do contribute to greater security of supply and stability of terms, it is necessary to ask whether the mechanisms of special relationships or these U.S. relationships with these particular countries offer the best, worst or only way to secure access to oil in the prevailing international environment? What is the impact of such relationships on the domestic Saudi and Iranian political systems? If the effects are negative, is short-term security of supply purchased at the expense of jeopardizing longer term security of supply? Does the United States-Saudi relationship and the United States-Iranian relationship result in greater independence/reduced vulnerability for the United States or merely greater dependence on these sources or a more balanced interdependence occasioned by the multiplication of ties created within the special relationship? What is the impact of these relationships on third parties who are of interest to the United States for a variety of reasons—U.S. allies, non-oil LDC's other producers and the U.S.S.R.?

Finally, what is the implication of the United States having simultaneous "special relationships" with both these countries?

Strategy

Part II is devoted to a study of a past attempt to create a special relationship between a developed country (France) and an LDC raw materials producer (Algeria). In an analysis of the relationship established between France and Algeria in the mid-sixties, are there lessons for current special relationships, their durability and the degree to which they can be mechanisms of access to raw materials?

Part III traces the evolution of U.S. relations with Saudi Arabia. This is followed by a detailed analysis of the existing and future economic, social, political and international developments of Saudi Arabia with a view toward suggesting the variety of factors which will influence Saudi decisions regarding access to oil for the United States and other consuming countries.

Included here is an evaluation of the interaction between the special relationship and Saudi oil policy with a view toward evaluating the impact of the special relationship on actual Saudi behavior. In addition, the Saudi interests to be served via the United States-Saudi relationship can be analyzed and the Saudi perception of the commitments it has undertaken in exchange for U.S. undertakings can be set against U.S. perceptions of the relationship and the commitments the United States believes it has undertaken.

A similar analysis for Iran follows in section IV.

Section V evaluates the special relationship mechanism against possible alternatives and/or supplements, and, in the light of the total analysis, suggests the implications for U.S. policy.

PART II.—THE FRANCO-ALGERIAN EXAMPLE, 1962–73

I. SPECIAL RELATIONSHIP BY DESIGN

Introduction

The Franco-Algerian relationship was grounded in the French desire to maintain access to Algerian oil and Algeria's willingness to accept that as a precondition of political independence. The question of access to Algerian oil was complicated by domestic political developments in each country, the broad range of interests which became involved, and the international goals and objectives of each country. The formal relationship was eventually undermined by changes in the international environment.

That there is a special relationship between France and Algeria based on a common language and long historical association is true and it endures. That it influenced French access to Algerian oil or enhanced security of supply is less apparent. In any event the Franco-Algerian example as a case study in the use of a special relationship as a mechanism for securing access to oil may be illustrative.

Historical Development

In the historical development of Franco-Algerian relations there are already indications of the later relationship and the problems associated with it. When the French landed on the Algerian coast in 1830, they occupied and controlled no more than that coastal strip. Only in 1857 was all of Algeria occupied and only in 1880 was Algeria considered "pacified." Despite the fact that it took 50 years to extend French control over the entire area, from the 1830's, various French decrees proclaimed Algeria an integral part of metropolitan France.

That claim was based, in part, on the large number of French and European settlers in Algeria (the colons), and the role they came to play in Algerian developments. When the French arrived in Algeria, it was administered by Turkish rulers as part of the Ottoman Empire. These forces were expelled and the colons increasingly created and dominated Algeria's economic, cultural, and political life. They became a force in their own right, apart from the metropolitan country and they guarded their privileges jealously. Islamic influence was minimized, French was made the official langauge and the educational system was designed to foster the French language and culture.

In spite of apparently limited educational and other opportunities for Algerians, enough of the French language, education, and culture had filtered throughout Algerian society by the early 1920's to inspire early Algerian nationalists with ideas of self-determination and political equality. World War I and the peace settlement reinforced the attraction of these ideas, and Algerian service in the French military argued for rights equal to the sacrifices Algerians had made in the war effort.

These early nationalists however, were essentially French in outlook and the title, "nationalist," is something of a misnomer. Their demands included the incorporation of Algeria in France, or French citizenship for Algerians without requiring them to renounce their Islamic heritage, or equal rights for Algeria's Muslim population. At this point it was not necessarily political independence that the nationalists sought.

Even if the French Government had been prepared to make concessions to the Algerian nationalists, concessions were made impossible by the vehement opposition of the colons. The colons were adamant in their refusal to consider any change in administration or status which threatened their economic and political privileges. In the interwar years, it became apparent that, from the point of view of the colons, change itself was threatening, with the result that little was accomplished in the way of assuaging nationalist sensibilities.

In the period after World War II, the French Government was so weakened by political instability and so preoccupied with postwar economic recovery, that the colons continued to hold the upper hand vis-a-vis both the Algerians and the French Government.

Under the circumstances, Algerian nationalism became increasingly radicalized. Control of the nationalist movement passed to those who despaired of any possibility for Muslim equality in a French Algeria and who saw in violence the only means of attaining the independence which now seemed essential.

The intensity of the 1954–62 war in Algeria reflected, on the one hand, the tenacity of a people who refused to be uprooted from their homes and privileges (and this apparently was the only outcome of change that the colons could envision), or to put themselves in a position where such an eventuality might materialize. On the other hand, the Algerian nationalists were convinced of the rightness of their cause and they equated independence with the sole opportunity for giving meaning and quality to the life of Algerians. The conflict could be nothing less than intense and total given the stakes each party believed to be involved.

On November 1, 1954, the Algerian war began. By 1956, it is generally agreed, the French military had succeeded in turning the battle in favor of France. But the war continued now taking the form of sporadic acts of terrorism. By 1958, it was mainly only the colons and some of the French military who were prepared to continue the struggle. When the beleagured French Government wavered, they wreaked havoc in the French political system raised the specter of a military coup d'etat in France and returned Gen. Charles de Gaulle to political power.

Algeria was a prime example of what later became a more common postwar phenomenon: Military victory no longer equated with political victory. The Algerians did not have to win militarily to defeat France politically; they merely had to continue the effort in such a way as to keep world attention focused on Algeria. The war was successfully and conclusively waged by the Algerian nationalists on the diplomatic/political front—in war-weary Paris, in the councils of NATO, in the 1955 conference of the nonaligned, less developed countries (LDC's), and in the LDC-dominated United Nations General Assembly.

That General de Gaulle came to oppose the colons, who had been instrumental in returning him to power, and to bring the war to an end was a function of his sensitivity to the political dimension of the struggle and the different international role he envisaged for France. In 1961, de Gaulle offered the French and the Algerians a choice. As a result of the referendum the French recognized the right of the people of Algeria to choose their political future; the Algerians opted for independence and close cooperation with France. In spite of continued resistance from the colons, Algeria became independent in July 1962; by October 1962, some 800,000 colons fled the chaos they had no small part in creating.

The initial effect of the long period of colonial rule was to make a postindependence relationship with France essential. Algeria depended on French administrators and technicians; when the colons left, association with the French Government was vital.

As a result, the Algerian attitude toward France was one of ambivalence—a recognition of Algeria's continuing need for cooperation with France and a resentment of that need, which Algerians attributed to colonial policies and the inadequate preparation they had received under colonial rule. The conflicting and contrary pulls of this ambivalence continue to be in evidence in Franco-Algerian relations.

In addition, independence came as a result of a protracted struggle which could not help but color relations between the two countries. The intensity of the conflict could be ascribed to the colons, but Franco-Algerian relations would always be affected by the image and memories of the colonial past.

Finally, of some importance to later developments in Franco-Algerian relations, was the fact that, as a result of the struggle for independence, Algeria became a symbol to the less-developed countries of all efforts, anywhere, to throw off colonial oppression in all its myriad forms.

The Evian Declarations

The Evian declarations of March 1962, brought to a conclusion the bitter, 8-year struggle for Algerian independence. The basis for the settlement was De Gaulle's willingness to grant Algerian independence in exchange for continued access to Algerian oil and nuclear test sites.

The Evian declarations, and subsequent cooperation agreements, marked a deliberate attempt to formalize and institutionalize the Franco-Algerian relationship—recognizing, reflecting, and building upon the special ties developed during the previous 130 years and the common needs and interests derived from that—but now outside the colonial context. Atop the less formal ties existing between Algeria and France, Evian constructed a formal, bilateral, government-to-government relationship and both were aspects of the Franco-Algerian special relationship.

The initial concern of the agreement was to protect the civil rights of French citizens and the property rights of French enterprises in Algeria. The Algerians committed themselves to guarantee these.

The settlement also stipulated that Algeria would remain in the franc currency zone, facilitating Franco-Algerian trade. In transactions between themselves, it was not necessary to use hard currency reserves. The promise of preferential trading arrangements was also offered in the Evian declarations.

With regard to the military, all French troops would be withdrawn by the end of a 3-year period. However, Algeria agreed to lease to

France the Mers-El-Keber military base for 15 years. Algeria also accorded France the use of, "military airfields, terrain, sites, and installations." The military sections of the agreement were of considerable importance to France; France had embarked on a nuclear weapons development program which required continued French access to the Saharan testing grounds.

In addition, the accord provided for the creation of a joint Franco-Algerian technical body to undertake cooperative ventures in the exploitation of Saharan minerals, including oil. The new organization would give advice on Algerian draft bills and regulations pertaining to minerals exploitation in Algeria and would also assess all requests for mining concessions.

These functions obviously gave France considerable influence in determining the terms of access to Algeria's natural resources and a major voice in deciding which companies would have access. It was further stipulated that, for a period of 6 years, in the event that equal bids were received for any particular minerals project, preference should be given to French companies. At the same time, France adopted domestic policies which resulted in preferential access for franc zone, largely Algerian, oil to the French market.

In effect, by the terms of the agreement at least, France succeeded in: (1) safeguarding the position of Europeans in Algeria; (2) securing access to the military facilities required for the continued development of French nuclear weapons; and, (3) retaining a dominant role in the exploitation of Saharan oil.

The Algerians, practically defeated militarily, nevertheless: (1) gained independence; (2) avoided a French plan to establish a federal political structure in Algeria; (3) secured a phased withdrawal of French troops; (4) gained preferential access to the French oil market; and (5) obtained a French commitment to provide substantial amounts of technical, cultural, and financial assistance.

Oil

THE 1965 OIL AGREEMENT

The Evian declarations set a framework which was to be filled in by subsequent agreement. In July 1965, a 5-year petroleum accord was concluded by the two countries, subjecting the French companies, for the first time, to a regime negotiated and agreed solely by the two governments. At the same time, all non-French foreign oil companies were "invited" to terminate their operations in Algeria—none of them did so at this time.

In return for: (1) the privileged position accorded the French Government regarding French influence on Algerian rules and regulations for minerals exploitation; (2) the preference to be given French companies; and (3) secure access to oil which could be purchased without using hard currency reserves, a factor of some importance in 1965, the French Government committed the French oil producing companies, controlling about 60 percent of Algerian production, as follows:

One: Existing fields, that is, those under development and production, would remain in the hands of the French companies unchanged except that such rights as were formally held by the colony were turned over to the Algerian Republic.

Two: All future rights for oil and gas exploration were vested in a joint French-Algerian body, Ascoop.

Three: The companies, in turn, would calculate the taxes owed to Algeria on the basis of a posted price agreed to by the two governments.

Four: The companies would undertake to finance, at their own risk, exploration and development activities in Algeria.

Five: The companies would repatriate to Algeria a substantial portion of the profits derived from the sale of Algerian oil abroad.

While these provisions appear tame from the perspective of post-1973 oil developments, in 1965, it is probably fair to say that they constituted an innovation in the relations between oil companies and a producing government. Algeria was assured of a secure market for its oil exports which again in the context of 1965, when the oil supply/demand situation did not favor producers as it does today, was of considerable importance to Algeria. But because the regime was established by the two governments, it received something less than the total commitment of the companies—in spite of the fact that the French Government was a substantial shareholder in one and sole owner of the other.

With regard to price, or the terms of access, it may be that France paid more for Algerian oil (but not in hard currency) than for supplies from other sources. Oil arrangements came to be associated with the full range of Franco-Algerian relations—wine exports, Algerian workers in France, French social security payments to Algerians, et cetera—with difficulties or advantages in any particular area reflecting on the others.

The price of oil then included the price of French aid and other Franco-Algerian dealings. Of course the factors motivating French assistance were broader than oil and it may have been that France would have supplied the assistance regardless of oil; that is, oil was merely an additional bonus to be derived from an aid program which had several motivations—economic and political. Not all aid represents the equivalent of higher oil prices, but some proportion might be so attributed.

In terms of the companies, all indications are that they did not receive a price discount on Algerian oil. In fact they may have paid a premium beyond that stemming from the high quality and favorable location of Algerian oil, in terms of price and in terms of the financial implications of restrictions on profit repatriation and required new investments.

The French Government was assured of franc zone oil; the Algerians received a guaranteed market for their oil and large French aid commitments for oil exploration and industrialization. The companies were subject to an innovative regime in which they may have had little confidence.

REVISION OF THE 1965 AGREEMENT

Oil issues were among the most contentious ones in Franco-Algerian relations and it was on these issues that the formal special relationship broke down. The Algerians complained of inadequate exploration activity. They also suspected that the French companies were getting around the repatriation-to-Algeria requirements through the transfer price mechanism. By 1969, when the countries began negotiating a revision of the 1965 accord, the Algerians were also pressing for an increase in the posted price.

To assess the impact of the Franco-Algerian special relationship on oil issues, an analysis of events affecting the non-French oil companies is useful. In 1967, in response to the Arab-Israeli war, the Algerian Government placed the operations of American oil companies under government control. In addition, when Sinclair merged with Atlantic Richfield, its concession in Algeria was canceled. In 1968, Algeria nationalized all companies, including French companies, involved in the internal distribution of oil and gas products.

In April 1970, the Algerian Government informed the non-French oil producing companies that they must relinquish to Algeria a majority interest in their operations or sell out altogether. In June 1970, the assets of Shell, Phillips, Elwerth (West German), and an Italian company were nationalized, followed by Mobil and Newmont Overseas in November. Almost all U.S. companies in Algeria were now nationalized; the only foreign producing companies in Algeria by 1971, were Getty, and the French companies, CFP and Elf-ERAP.

The Algerians were to be more circumspect in their dealings with the French. In July 1970, the Algerian Government notified CFP and Elf-ERAP that the posted price had been increased from $2.08 to $2.85 a barrel, retroactive to January 1, 1970. The Algerians also demanded a majority position in joint French-Algerian operations; the French Government rejected both demands and Algeria did not impose them at this time. Instead broad government-to-government negotiations were initiated to deal with the entire range of issues concerning Franco-Algerian relations—that is, oil, workers, wine exports, et cetera, and these talks continued through February 1971.

Both the French and the Algerians demonstrated some restraint in the negotiations; there appeared to be an unwillingness to push differences to the breaking point. At the same time, France tried to mobilize other facets of the relationship to affect the oil issue. In October 1970, the French Government relaxed the restrictions on French refiners which had forced them to give preference to oil imports from the franc zone. France also suspended wine imports from Algeria. The Organization for Industrial Cooperation was ended in January 1971.

Changes in the international energy and political environment undermined the French position. The oil supply/demand situation was changing in favor of the oil producing countries. Rapid economic growth in the United States, Western Europe and Japan and the entry of the United States into the international oil market as a major purchaser post-1970, resulted in a rapid increase in oil-import demand. The transition from a buyers' to a sellers' market was an important factor permitting the oil producing countries to wrest control of their oil resources from the international oil companies. Algeria's neighbor, Libya was an early example of the ability of the oil producers to redistribute the benefits of oil exploitation in their favor.

The message was not lost on the Algerians who grew increasingly impatient with the French Government's delays, the French presumption that posted prices must be agreed by both countries, and French efforts to use the nonoil aspects of the Franco-Algerian relationship as bargaining levers vis-a-vis Algeria.

The achievement of control over oil resources was a longstanding LDC goal; in LDC thinking control of indigenous resources was a necessary condition for economic independence and development. Algeria, a leader among LDC's, would not remain unaffected by these considerations. The international environment was not conducive to a continuation of Franco-Algerian oil relations on the same terms that had prevailed in the past.

POSTNATIONALIZATION DEVELOPMENTS

On February 24, 1971, Algeria unilaterally assumed a 51-percent interest in the French oil companies operating in Algeria. The assumption of a 51-percent share had an element of sleight of hand to it. On the one hand an Algerian 51-percent interest looked like an Algerian act of moderation, given the total nationalization of the non-French oil producing companies. On the other hand, the difference was merely cosmetic; for controlling the operations of a company 51 percent is quite as effective as 100 percent. In fact, a determined government could control company operations with no equity participation at all. The remaining 49 percent in French hands had symbolic value to the French and Algerians, desiring clear legal title to the oil and the avoidance of French court proceedings against Algerian oil sales, agreed.

As a result of the 1967–68 and 1970–71 nationalizations, Sonatrach, the Algerian state oil company established in 1963, controlled approximately 80 percent of oil production and 100 percent of internal distribution of Algerian oil.

With the nationalization, France announced that the special relationship was terminated and instituted an embargo of Algerian oil; French imports fell to 25 percent of the previous level. The embargo was defeated by the development of a tighter oil supply/demand situation, enabling Algeria to sell its oil elsewhere in spite of threatened French legal action.

With the end of the formal special relationship, France indicated that all bilateral issues between the two countries, would be dealt with individually. In addition, the French Government returned the responsibility for Franco-Algerian oil relations to the companies. In the summer and fall of 1971, settlements were negotiated with CFP and Elf-ERAP which allowed the companies to continue operations in Algeria. France consequently lifted its embargo on Algerian oil.

Algeria was determined to do as well vis-a-vis the French companies as OPEC was doing in regard to the international oil companies generally. As a leader of LDC's, Algeria could do no less. Getty, which came into Algeria on terms more favorable to Algeria and more reflective of evolving oil company relations apparently continued operations through the 1970–71 nationalizations.

Following the nationalizations, Algeria sought a new modus vivendi with new markets and the international oil companies. In April 1971, a new oil law set out the terms under which foreign companies could operate in Algeria, now only in partnership with Sonatrach. In 1972–73, oil sales contracts of 3 to 5 years' duration were negotiated with

Exxon, Gulf, Commonwealth Oil Refining, Sun Oil, Phillips, Mobil, Petrolbras (Brazil) and Poland.

Algeria remained dependent on the industrialized countries for markets and technical expertise. In addition, having assumed control of the domestic refining industry, Algeria was eager to find markets for oil products, capturing the value added in the further processing of crude oil. In 1972, Algeria offered to guarantee regular and stable oil supplies to the European Community (EC) in return for an EC-Algeria association agreement. The oil guarantee was linked to the EC's opening its market to Algeria's refined products, the freer movement of Algerian workers throughout the Community and greater Community purchases of Algerian wine. In the event, the Community did not agree to accept Algerian oil products in quantities satisfactory to Algeria.

Post 1973, the Algerians were probably less interested in extending guarantees; the balance of power had shifted in favor of the oil-producing countries and the prospects for increasing oil prices may have made the Algerians reluctant to bind themselves to an international agreement. Moreover, the change from a buyers' to a sellers' market made diversification of the markets for Algeria's oil easily attainable—consumers would need to buy all oil available everywhere.

To reverse the declining trend in oil production, Sonatrach turned to the techical expertise of the international oil companies. Sonatrach held talks with 20 oil companies in January 1973, with a view toward forming joint exploration ventures. That same month agreement was reached with Petrobras, followed by similar agreements with Sun Oil, Total-Algeris (CFP), Hispanoil (Spain), Deminex (West Germany) and Amoco.

Algeria has followed OPEC's pricing policies, indeed Algeria has been in the forefront of those producers demanding even higher oil prices. While Algeria indicated that it would participate in the 1973 OPEC oil embargo and production curtailment instituted in response to the Arab-Israeli war, the Algerians went to great lengths to assure France that its oil supplies would not be affected.

The effort to reassure France suggests that something of the special relationship continues to function, even if in ways not always anticipated by the participants. CFP-Sonatrach relations have been exceptionally good. In December 1974, Sonatrach and CFP agreed to activate the second 5-year term of their 1971 oil agreement. In addition, the two companies reached agreement on the expansion of the area being worked by Total-Algerie and a new agreement relating to joint exploration offshore Algeria was concluded. Elf-ERAP, however, elected not to activate the second half of its 10-year agreement, citing the high cost of Algerian oil as the cause and stating that it would prefer a "normal commercial agreement" to a continuation of the 1971 agreement.

On the level of the French and Algerian Governments, oil relations were sometimes the source of conflict and sometimes the reflection of conflict in other areas of Franco-Algerian relations. In 1969, when the 1965 oil agreement came up for renewal, the Algerians refrained from imposing a settlement on the French companies. There is some indication that the 1970 nationalizations of the non-French operating companies were intended to warn the French Government that a similar fate could await CFP and Elf-ERAP. The Algerians went along with the French Government's demands for a continued French equity interest in Algerian oil. Algeria was responsive and cautious but determined to have its way in its oil dealings with France.

On a more practical level the minority partner (the French companies) continued to exercise influence by dint of its technical and managerial control. But by 1970-71 the international situation strongly favored the Algerian position. Moreover, as a leader of the less developed countries, Algeria was compelled to seize the opportunity now offered to secure control of its indigenous resources and the economic independence and opportunities implied in doing so. If the international environment undermined the persuasive influence of the special relationship, internal political developments in both countries also influenced Franco-Algerian relations.

Algeria

The Evian settlement and cooperation with France following the debilitating war for independence were more than a convenience; cooperation was essential if Algeria was to avoid chaos. With the departure of the French, there was a real prospect for total administrative and economic collapse. French technical assistance, bureaucrats, teachers and aid remained essential, fueling the ambivalent attitude Algerians held regarding France.

In addition, the problems of administration and government were compounded by the outbreak of civil war in Algeria. The desire for independence and the revolutionary struggle had unified a disparate group of forces and interests in the National Liberation Front (FLN). Once the war with France was concluded and independence achieved, the primary basis for unity evaporated. The exigencies of wartime had made it possible to overlook the fact that there was no program and no agreement on the elements of a program for national development, direction and goals.

The war itself had contributed to the divisiveness of Algerian politics by creating several competing centers of power. There were the so-called historic leaders, including Ahmed Ben Bella, who had spent most of the war in French prisons. There was also the Government Provisoire de la Republic Algerienne (GPRA), the Algerian provisional government established in 1958.

The military also was divided. For the prosecution of the war effort the country had been divided into wilaya or military districts. Wilaya military commanders had considerable autonomy and a great deal of local influence which they were reluctant to relinquish to a central government in which they did not have a major voice. In addition, the general staff of the National Liberation Army (ALN), had spent a good part of the war in Tunisia and Morocco where French border forces prevented their greater participation in the war for independence.

Add to these structural divisions, existing personal and ideological rivalries and the chaotic condition of post-independence, Algerian politics is evident. In the event, Ben Bella outmaneuvered the GPRA forces and, with the assistance of the ALN led by Colonel Boumedienne, forcibly subdued the wilaya commanders. He then proceeded to extend his dominance over all aspects of the Algerian political system.

However, Algerian politics continued to be dominated by factions often formed around a leading personality. The mass of Algerians, disappointed by the outbreak of civil war and the ensuing damage inflicted on Algerians by Algerians, withdrew into political apathy. Institutional developments atrophied with the unwillingness to countenance the development of institutions which might serve as a basis of political support for competing factions.

In the course of solidifying his domestic political position, Ben Bella played the numerous factions off against each other, finally alienating most of them. Without the institutional development which might have mobilized large numbers of Algerians to serve as a viable alternative source of political support, Ben Bella increasingly relied on the support of political support for a cometing faction.

As Ben Bella tried to broaden his base of political support beyond the military, he came to rely on the leftist forces—the Algerian Communist Party (PCA) and the militant labor organization (UGTA). Whatever the sincerity of his socialist pronouncements, the leftist forces took him at his word and pushed him to the left.

With a great many vacated French properties, including factories and some of the best agricultural land, the initial steps toward socialism could be achieved easily and painlessly at the expense of foreigners. At this point socialism involved no more than the takeover of the vacated French facilities by Algerian workers and farmers. The Tripoli program (1962) suggested that Algeria was to be a socialist state; the March 1963 decrees regarding the vacated property were the proof.

This neatly dovetailed with international developments. Algeria was born of an extended revolutionary struggle for independence and it came to symbolize all similar efforts anywhere. Ben Bella, having already participated in the Third World movement as part of the diplomatic/political battle for independence, easily turned his attention from the chaotic domestic arena to international affairs.

He envisaged Algeria as a leader of a united Third World bloc. He focused his attention on Africa on the assumption that Algerian leadership in Africa would give Algeria considerable influence over the entire Third World. Colonialism and capitalism were interrelated in the LDC mind and Third World leadership required anti-Westernism, or at a minimum, neutrality, and a dedication to socialism.

With the increasing socialist bent of the regime and the aspiration to Third World leadership based in a common Algerian-LDC commitment to oppose imperialism in all its forms, the association with France was something of an embarrassment. The relationship was downplayed lest it taint Algeria's revolutionary and socialist image.

At the same time, there were continuous harangues demanding additional French assistance. From the perspective of the Algerians their demands were legitimate; France owed Algeria assistance as compensation for past injustices and the lack of development they attributed to colonial rule.

In 1965, when Ben Bella attempted to bring the military under his control, Colonel Boumedienne staged a coup d'etat which replaced Ben Bella with a Revolutionary Command Council in June. The Franco-Algerian relationship continued as before, with both sides eager to demonstrate that the solidarity of the relationship did not depend on a single individual. The petroleum accord negotiated under Ben Bella's regime was adopted and implemented by Boumedienne's and within five weeks of the coup, France and Algeria signed a 15-year cooperation agreement.

Yet there were at least two changes in the post-coup regime which inevitably had a significant impact on Franco-Algerian relations. First, Boumedienne's nationalism was to prove far more unsettling in Franco-Algerian relations than Ben Bella's socialism. Expressed in the form of the 1966, 1968, 1970–71 nationalizations, nationalism was an irritant in relations between the two countries.

In addition, Algerian nationalism dictated national independence which, in turn, required a diversification of Algeria's external relations. In 1970, an economic and technical assistance agreement was signed with Belgium; in April 1970, a scientific and cultural agreement was concluded with Poland. A Soviet-Algerian Permanent Committee for Economic, Scientific, and Technical Cooperation was established and ties to other European countries were cultivated.

Second, the change in leadership from Ben Bella to Boumedienne also reoriented Algeria's focus of attention in regional relations. Under Boumedienne attention turned from Black Africa in the south, to the Arabs in the east. The Arab-Israeli conflict thus came to strain Franco-Algerian relations periodically. French support vis-a-vis Tunisia and/or Morocco is also at times a sore point. Finally, the increasing focus on the Arab countries placed Algeria firmly in OPEC and OAPEC, with obvious implications for Algeria's oil policy vis-a-vis France and the French companies.

FRANCE

The return of General de Gaulle to political power in France had significant implications for ending the Algerian conflict and the nature of the postindependence Franco-Algerian relationship.

His vision for France and Europe, if the latter accepted it, included a major international role for France—and Europe—free of U.S. influence. In any event, France was to be a power and leader in its own right. Consistent with this desire was the development of leadership and influence in the newly emerging countries. French influence in the LDC's, in turn, would enhance the French position vis-a-vis the Anglo-Saxon countries; that is, the United States and the United Kingdom.

For de Gaulle then, Algeria was a festering wound threatening his vision of France's international role, particularly among the LDC's and through them, with the developed countries. Resolution of the conflict became more important than any possible benefits to be derived from holding on in Algeria.

With the conclusion of the war and Algerian independence in 1962, De Gaulle's view required that Franco-Algerian relations continue. Algeria had become a symbol to the LDCs, and by linking France to it Algeria was to serve as De Gaulle's, "narrow door into the Third World." Algeria was to be a test case, a model of French efforts and intentions regarding the LDC's and an example of the benefits of cooperation with France.

There were, of course, other interests involved. There remained a sizable number of Frenchmen in Algeria. Access to the Saharan testing grounds remained essential. French investments in Algerian oil approached $10 billion. Moreover, through the sixties De Gaulle was engaged in a running battle with the United States regarding international monetary reserves and the U.S. balance of payments deficits which increased the desirability of franc zone oil. De Gaulle's hopes for France and its place in the world disposed him toward institutionalizing the relationship with Algeria.

Throughout the sixties, the ties were multiplied. In December 1967, a military assistance agreement was signed. Trade agreements were negotiated. Training facilities were established and staffed with French instructors; Algerian students studied in France. French bureaucrats continued to be seconded for service in Algeria. In spite of continuing frictions in the relations between the two countries, the formal special relationship remained intact as long as General de Gaulle dominated French politics.

Conclusion

The attempt to institutionalize the Franco-Algerian relationship through the provisions of the Evian declarations was undermined by political developments in each country and in the international environment.

Among the primary objectives of Evian had been the French interest in safeguarding the civil and property rights of French citizens in Algeria. In fact this section of the agreement was unenforceable once the colons abandoned their Algerian holdings.

The subsequent Algerian occupation of the vacated property represented, from the French perspective, a violation of the Evian settlement. From the Algerian perspective, the vacated property was abandoned and therefore, available, while compensation to the imperialists was inconsistent with the image Algeria was trying to project internationally.

In this respect, at least, Evian was stillborn; other interests, however, kept the special relationship functioning. In effect, France continued to demand compensation for French property in a rather desultory way, while maintaining the relationship for other, perhaps more important ends; that is, oil, the Saharan testing grounds and the "narrow door to the Third World." For the narrow door to the Third World and continued preferential access to Algerian resources, the French Government accepted the violation of French property rights.

From the Algerian perspective, the relationship was necessary given Algeria's dependence on French administrators, trade, capital, technical assistance, employment opportunities in France, and French financial aid. It could easily be imagined that when the Algerians saw alternatives to the French, the inequality of the relationship would disappear and a great deal of French leverage vis-a-vis Algeria with it. Algerian ambivalence regarding France resulted in discontinuities in Algerian policy which caused strain in the government-to-government relationship.

The relationship was strained in a multitude of other ways, including an apparent incompatibility in systems of government and international goals. Algeria's internal political development, and the role it sought to play in international affairs, militated against too close or obvious a relationship with France, while French international objectives required a close and public relationship with Algeria.

The continuing nationalizations which gave credence to Algeria's socialism, further violated the rights of foreign property owners. In addition, Ben Bella's socialism and perhaps even more, Boumedienne's nationalism led Algeria to diversify its international relationships.

From the perspective of French hopes for the "narrow door," the continuous Algerian harangues demanding additional French assistance as if it were due Algeria for the past injustices suffered at the hands of the French, rankled and did not suggest to the other developing countries the types of arrangements of equality and mutual benefits possible through cooperation with France that the French wanted to demonstrate.

In addition, it is important to note the role played by General de Gaulle in engineering and maintaining the formal, special relationship with Algeria. It was de Gaulle's vision of France's place in the world that gave Algeria importance either as the "narrow door," or as the owner of the Saharan testing ground and oil. As long as de Gaulle perceived Algeria to be of some importance in terms of wider French interests, the formal relationship persisted. When de Gaulle left the French political scene, there was less emphasis on de Gaulle's particular vision for France and less tolerance for Algeria's persistent demands.

With regard to oil, the Evian settlement, confirmed by the 1965 oil accord, gave France a privileged place in Algerian oil and gas affairs. The French had considerable influence over the rules and regulations regarding minerals exploitation in Algeria and a voice in determining which foreign companies would have access to Algeria's resources. At this time, the American companies complained that they were being squeezed out of Algeria by the French and in 1965 they were "invited" to leave the country.

In return, the French compelled their refiners to purchase oil from the franc zone, effectively giving Algerian crude preferential access to the French market. In addition, the French Government determined the Algerian oil regime under which the French companies would operate in Algeria, committing them to high prices, large repatriation (to Algeria) requirements and additional investment in Algerian resources.

By 1969–70, the oil demand/supply situation was transformed from one of adequate supply to one of tight supply. In addition, OPEC negotiations with the companies in 1971–72, suggested that the time was opportune for producer countries to assume greater control over their resources and to redistribute the benefits of oil exploitation in their favor. Algerian nationalism demanded that Algeria do at least as well as OPEC generally.

When in 1970, the French Government rejected Algeria's demand for a majority interest in the joint French-Algerian ventures, the Algerians did not impose a settlement. The non-French companies, however, were nationalized completely.

The Franco-Algerian talks continued for over a year and it seems that each side demonstrated considerable restraint and consciously tried to refrain from pushing their differences to the breaking point.

But the situation in 1971, was sufficiently different from the situation in 1962 and 1965, to weaken the attractiveness of the formal special relationship from both the French and Algerian viewpoints. For France, General de Gaulle was no longer in power and even if the new French Government still felt the need for a "narrow door" it was increasingly apparent that Algeria would not serve that role. The importance of the military facilities had declined and De Gaulle returned the Mers-El-Keber base before the expiration of the lease. In effect, for France, the single most important remaining issue was oil and when that was gone the formal, special relationship was terminated.

For Algeria, the development of a tight oil supply situation meant that Algeria was no longer dependent on preferential access to French markets; all oil available for world trade would find a ready market. And while French manipulation of the nonoil facets of the special relationship to influence the Algerian position on oil probably induced an element of caution into Algerian calculations, Algeria could do no less than other oil producers were doing vis-a-vis the oil companies.

Algerian treatment of the French companies was little better than the treatment accorded non-French companies. In terms of control of company operations, 51 percent will suffice; but the remaining 49 percent was important to the French companies which continued to operate the fields. Given Algeria's continuing need for technical assistance and expertise, Algeria invited other foreign oil companies into the country on terms no more onerous than those imposed on CFP and Elf-ERAP. But when the French Government stepped out of oil affairs, CFP and Elf-ERAP continued to operate in Algeria on the basis of new agreements reached between the companies and the Algerian Government. Elf subsequently terminated its agreement with Algeria.

The persuasive effects of the formal special relationship depended on several factors, which by 1971 were much less in evidence than in 1962: continued Algerian dependence on French assistance and markets, the French desire to purchase franc zone oil, broader French foreign policy goals, and the presence of General de Gaulle. By 1971, international and internal political and economic developments undermined the persuasive power of the formal relationship and when Algerian and French interests diverged, France terminated the relationship.

At the same time, an informal network of ties built up over the years continues to function. A less formal special relationship based on a common language, culture, legal system and education, continues to be a factor in Algerian calculations, as in 1973, when Algeria assured the French that oil supplies would not be affected by the OAPEC embargo. In addition, a special relationship exists between the companies, CFP and Sonatrach.

In conclusion, the special relationship itself was dependent on a range of supportive factors which gave it persuasive influence; when these faded in importance, the core of the relationship—economics, language, culture—survived. It is genuine, it is mutual with France; it depends not on government-to-government formal undertakings but on a relationship which is "natural," serving neither to limit one nor the other's general political and economic horizons. Did the government-to-government relationship secure access to Algerian oil which France would not have received in the absence of the relationship? Probably not.

The Algerian example also demonstrates the very many factors, including the special relationship but not limited to it, which come to affect access to a producer's resources—domestic, economic and political developments, international goals and objectives, personalities and trends in more general international relations. The following detailed analyses of Saudi Arabia and Iran are therefore long but necessarily so. In fact they are essential if post-1973, the needs and objectives of producing countries will be increasingly important determinants of access to oil.

PART III.—SAUDI ARABIA

I. HISTORICAL DEVELOPMENTS

INTRODUCTION

In Saudi Arabia's history one finds expression of the tribal and traditional basis of Saudi society, the role of the Saud ruling family and Saudi adherence to orthodox Islam without which it will be impossible for Westerners to understand this country of such consequence to the continued availability of adequate oil supplies in world trade. Such an understanding is also a prerequisite for comprehending the effects and direction of change in Saudi Arabia. In addition, in the history of Saudi development there is evidence of past contacts with the West which will continue to have a bearing on future relations and access to Saudi oil.

THE HOUSE OF SAUD

In the early 18th century the Sauds represented one family among a multiplicity of families and tribes, each of which ruled various, limited parts of the Arabian peninsula. In the middle of the century, Mohammed Ibn Saud, the founder of the current dynasty, became an adherent of the puritanical Wahhabi sect of Sunni Islam. Uniting Bedouin forces with religious fervor, he extended his influence throughout the central plateau region, the Nejd, through military conquest, marriages and alliances. By the early 19th century his descendents had extended the Saudi-Wahhabi empire from the Red Sea to the Gulf and from Yemen to the gates of Damascus.

The Ottomans, who had controlled the Red Sea coastal region, the Hejaz and Asir, since the 16th century responded to the Saudi challenge to their position. By 1818, they had reduced the Sauds to a small emirate in the Nejd under Egyptian suzerainty. The British, allied with the Ottomans at this time, began to extend their influence around the periphery of the Arabian Sea and Gulf region.

In the Nejd, the Ottomans played the rival families and tribes against each other, supporting particularly those groups opposed to the Sauds. The history of the Nejd in the 19th century is one of incessant feuding and warfare among the rival families and tribal units. By the middle of the century the Sauds had reasserted their authority over much of the area only to be reduced again when feuding within the family resulted in the disintegration of the Saudi realm. In 1891, the powerful Rashid family forced the Sauds into exile in Kuwait.

The modern history of Saudi Arabia can be traced to the opening years of this century and the efforts of Abd al-Aziz Ibn Saud (generally known as Ibn Saud), to recapture the Nejd and unify the entire peninsula under Saudi rule. In 1902, he captured Riyadh and his success rallied neighboring Bedouin tribes to the Saudi cause. Throughout 1902-04 Ibn Saud extended his influence in the Nejd. By 1906 Saudi control of the Nejd was reestablished; by 1913 Saudi control of the Gulf province of al-Hasa was secured.

The families and tribes existing in areas where the Sauds extended their control were not eliminated; this was not the way of the desert. Instead they were required simply to acknowledge their allegiance to the House of Saud. At times this was accomplished by military means or through marriage alliances. In addition, success itself rallied others to the Saudi side.

But in Wahhabi doctrine and the role of the Sauds in propagating and defending it, Ibn Saud found a more effective basis for securing loyalty and support and an effective means of uniting all the tribes and families in one religious grouping. Wahhabis alone were viewed as true Moslems and they must stand together. The Ikhwan (brethren) movement united all believers regardless of other affiliations and Ibn Saud assumed the role of imam (religious leader). The history of the Saud family and the unification of the peninsula cannot be separated from the history of Wahhabism.

The limits of Saudi expansion were set by British interests in the Gulf and southern Arabia. However, as World War I approached and with the British now opposed to the Ottomans, the Saudis were encouraged to oppose those forces in Arabia still alined with the Ottoman Empire. In 1918, the Sauds routed the Rashids and extended their control north of the Nejd.

The British, however, also supported the Hashemites in the Hejaz who had rebelled against their Ottoman overlords in 1916. The support of Hussein of the Hejaz was considered essential; the possibility that the Arabs would side with the Ottomans in a holy war against the West was considered to be a real one and one to be avoided. The British encouraged Arab nationalists in their efforts to free themselves from Ottoman rule and promised Arab independence after the war. The British courted both Ibn Saud (by allowing him a free hand in the peninsula outside the Hejaz) and Sherif Hussein (with promises of Arab independence), the two rulers who would inevitably clash over supremacy in the Arabian peninsula and the larger world of Islam.

After the war the British secured thrones for two of Hussein's sons, one in Iraq and one in Transjordan. The Arabs believed they had been promised something different and relations between Hussein and the British continued to deteriorate. Ibn Saud found any northern claims he might harbor blocked by the British-created kingdoms and the Hashemites looked increasingly like rivals. When Hussein proclaimed himself caliph in 1924, making a bid for the leadership of the entire Islamic world, Ibn Saud had had enough and the British stood by as the Ikhwan Army moved into the Hejaz in 1924.

In 1926, Ibn Saud was crowned King of the Hejaz. In 1927, he was recognized as King of the Hejaz and Nejd and its Dependencies. By 1932, the Sauds had reunified their domains and secured control of the area and the Kingdom of Saudi Arabia was proclaimed.[1]

---

[1] For a detailed account of the rise of the House of Saud see H. St. John Philby, "Saudi Arbia" (New York: ARNO Press, 1972 reprint of the 1955 edition).

Society

In effect, the Saud family became dominant among the many families, tribes and villages constituting Saudi Arabia. The traditional social structures were not destroyed nor was such destruction ever a goal. The Sauds are the dominant family and Arabia consists of families and tribes joined by common allegiance to the House of Saud.

Ties of religion, kinship, marriage, and tribal subsidies are the ones which continue to bind Saudi Arabia together. Ibn Saud had 40 sons and the royal family today may consist of as many as 5,000 people. Virtually every tribe has direct ties to the royal family, typically by way of marriage ties. Apparently most ties bind groups to the royal family rather than to each other and it is religion which binds the whole together. The King is imam and the sharia is the official law of the land.

The size of the population is not known for certain or at least is not a matter of public record. Estimates run from 3.5 to 8 million but it is generally agreed that the lower figure is closer to the mark and this population occupies an area equal to the area of the United States east of the Mississippi. The population remains largely rural and there is still a sizable nomadic or seminomadic component. The population is young; perhaps 50 percent is under 20 years of age. The literacy rate is estimated to be no more than 5 to 20 percent of the population. While the population is homogenous in terms of religion (Sunni Moslems), language (Arabic) and ethnicity there are regional and social differences.

In Asir on the southern Red Sea coast the people, representing perhaps 25 percent of the Saudi population, are engaged in settled farming. In the Hejaz, which was exposed to cosmopolitan influences, the population is largely urban and engaged in trade. The Eastern Province, containing the oil fields and some very good agricultural land is the richest province. The Nejd and Northern Frontier Province house the nomads and oasis dwellers and here economic developments have not progressed as rapidly as in the Eastern Province and the Hejaz.

Superimposed on these economic and occupational differences are cultural and political differences which actually take the form of differences between the Nejd on the one hand and the Hejaz on the other. The people of the Hejaz have considered themselves to be more sophisticated than the Bedouin Arabs of the Nejd. The Bedouin Arabs consider themselves the purest of all Arabs and the repository of Arab virtues. Under the Ottomans, the Hejaz attained a measure of political autonomy and self-government. The Nejd is the original base of the Saudi family and the heartland of Wahhabism; many government officials and the bulk of the army and police forces derive from the Nejd.[2]

A far more serious division within the society is emerging with the influx of foreign labor; perhaps 40 percent of the total population is foreign. Yemenis, Sudanese, Pakistanis, Indians, and Africans are represented. Egyptians and other Arabs staff the schools and the upper levels of the bureaucracy. Europeans and Americans are plentiful.

---

[2] David E. Long, "Saudi Arabia" (Beverly Hills, Calif.: Sage Publications, 1976), p. 11.

In general, there is great concern within the kingdom regarding the potential social and political influence of these people. The Saudis therefore, keep them on a tight rein, isolated, on short-term contracts and always subject to immediate deportation at the discretion of the regime. Within the foreign community there is resentment regarding their status and treatment in Arabia.

Modern Saudi administration emerged only in the 1950's. Although Ministries of Finance and Foreign Affairs were established in the 1930's and the Defense Ministry was created in 1944, it was only in 1953 that a Council of Ministers was established to assist the King in decisionmaking, although all decisions are ultimately his. It was only after Ibn Saud's death in 1953, that educational and social welfare measures were even initiated. It was only in 1958 that the finances of the royal household were separated from the government's treasury. In a very real sense the modern Saudi Government and administration came into its own only in the mid-sixties.

The point here is that the society remains very much as it always has been with three important implications. First, it is a society of which the West is very largely ignorant and the ability of Westerners to comprehend its messages, motivations, expectations and goals is dangerously limited given the importance of the country.

Second, it is this still traditional society which is now being subject to new stresses related to the inflow of oil money and foreigners.[3] Saudi Arabia's continued willingness to produce oil in quantities necessary to meet world oil demand will be influenced by the extent to which the huge revenues thereby generated are viewed by the Saudi regime as threatening to or supportive of the social fabric on which the regime rests.

Third, while the influence of the religious leaders has been curtailed, religion remains an essential factor in Saudi society and politics. No Saudi government can afford to neglect the religious force which enabled Ibn Saud to unite the peninsula and which continues to provide a source of legitimacy for the regime.

Oil, World War II, and Relations With the West

If the West is generally unfamiliar with Saudi Arabia, it is also true that until the discovery of oil in Arabia in 1938, Saudi Arabia (excluding the Hejaz) had very little contact with or knowledge of the world beyond the peninsula.

The contacts Ibn Saud had were with Britain. The British not only held a dominant position in the sheikdoms on the borders of the peninsula thereby limiting the extension of Saudi influence, but they also supported the rival Hashemites. While the British eventually left the Hashemites in the Hejaz to their fate at the hands of the Saudis it is likely that this abandonment symbolized to the Saudis British treachery more than British support for the Saudis. There were interminable border disputes as tribes found their access to traditional grazing areas in the north cut off by the British.

In the early 1930's, when the Standard Oil Co. of California (Socal) demonstrated an interest in obtaining a Saudi concession, Ibn Saud

---

[3] See Edward R. F. Sheehan, "The Epidemic of Money," The New York Times Magazine, (New York, Nov. 14, 1976).

may have been eager to see if his kingdom, like neighboring Bahrain, held oil riches and in the process to counter British influence. The American company was awarded a concession in 1933; oil in commercial quantities was discovered in 1938.

The company, the Arabian American Oil Co. (Aramco) eventually consisted of Socal (30 percent), Texaco (30 percent), Exxon (30 percent), and Mobil (10 percent). Aramco activities beyond oil—in community development, education and training of Saudi nationals, in building hospitals and health clinics, etc.[4]—secured for America a large measure of Saudi goodwill which preceded U.S. Government involvement in Saudi Arabia and which continues to this day.

Official U.S. Government involvement in Saudi Arabia dates from World War II. In 1943, the first American legation was established; it was raised to Embassy status in 1949. Ibn Saud's friendly neutrality was of great importance to the allied war effort, including the 1944 agreement permitting the United States to erect and maintain a major airbase in Dhahran in exchange for U.S. assistance in military training. In 1943, Saudi Arabia was made eligible for lend-lease assistance and various loans from Aramco and the U.S. Government (filtered through the United Kingdom) were essential to Ibn Saud for whom the war had closed off traditional sources of revenues: that is, the pilgrimage and oil exports.

The termination of the war witnessed a rapid and substantial increase in official U.S. involvement in Saudi Arabia.[5] In the military area, the Dhahran airbase agreement was extended for another 5 years in 1951, in exchange for an expanded military training program and Saudi eligibility for U.S. arms aid under the Military Assistance Act. In 1957, the agreement was continued for another 5 years and Saudi Arabia was clearly included in the list of Middle East countries eligible for U.S. assistance under the Eisenhower doctrine. In 1962, the airbase agreement was terminated by the Saudi regime, but a letter from President Kennedy assured Saudi Arabia of America's continued commitment to its independence and territorial integrity.

In addition, Americans played a major role in technical assistance and economic development projects. In 1951, Saudi Arabia participated in the Point Four program of technical assistance. The U.S. Geological Survey prepared water and mineral resources studies and the U.S. Army Corps of Engineers began an involvement in Arabia which continues to this day and involves the corps in development projects worth literally billions of dollars.

American assistance was enlisted in 1952. in the areas of finance, customs, and the budget; and with U.S. advice the Saudi Arabian Monetary Agency (the central bank) was established. Additional American assistance was enlisted in the formation of the Ministries of Agriculture, Education. and Communications.

In addition to this partial listing suggesting the extent of official U.S. involvement in Saudi Arabia. private American companies were involved in Saudi developments. With the coming of the increase in oil wealth post-1973. the participation of American companies in Saudi

---
[4] Arabian American Oil Company. Aramco Handbook: Oil in the Middle East (Dhahran. Saudi Arabia · Arabian American Oil Co., 1968).
[5] K S Twitchell, "Saudi Arabia: With an Account of the Development of Its Natural Resources" (Princeton, N J : Princeton University Press, 1958)

Arabia has become even more extensive and there may be as many as 30,000 American expatriates in Saudi Arabia.

The major complicating factor in United States-Saudi relations was—and is—U.S. support for Jewish immigration to Palestine and, later, U.S. support for the new Israeli nation. In the mid-fifties, also, Saudi internal developments briefly moved it closer to Nasser's Egypt and away from the United States. But this was a very brief Egyptian-Saudi rapprochment and the U.S. relationship remained intact in spite of the embarrassment caused to the Saudis by their close association with Israel's major supporter.

Relations with England and France were broken as a result of their participation in the 1956 Suez crisis. Relations with France were further complicated by Saudi opposition to the French position in Algeria. Diplomatic relations with France were resumed in 1962. Diplomatic relations with Britain were restored in 1963, but the United Kingdom-Saudi Buraimi oasis dispute remained unresolved. French and British assistance in the development of the Saudi military, along with U.S. aid was a characteristic goal of Saudi policy.

The Soviet Union and Communist ideology are considered anathema to the conservative and religious Saudi regime. Islam and Communist atheism are inconsistent and so is the Saudi traditional regime and Soviet support for Arab radicals.

In spite of U.S. support for Israel, the Aramco and official postwar experience, the presumed (by the Saudis) technological superiority of the United States and a common aversion to the spread of Soviet influence and Arab radicalism found the United States as the major foreign factor in Saudi Arabia. The connection probably did cause the Saudis difficulties with other Arab countries (although those difficulties would have materialized anyway).

Against the background of the relative unwillingness of the United States to involve itself elsewhere in the Middle East in the fifties, it must be assumed that oil and the dominant position of the American companies in Saudi oil contributed to official U.S. interest in Arabia. Except for Bahrain and Saudi Arabia, Middle East oil was dominated by the British. From the beginning then, the United States-Saudi relationship involved considerations of oil and it is unlikely that the Saudis fail to understand the connection.

II. ECONOMIC DEVELOPMENTS

INTRODUCTION

The issue of access to Saudi Arabia's oil involves the question of future Saudi production levels perhaps even more than the question of terms and price. In the near term, if world economic recovery should gather momentum, it is likely that the resulting oil import demand could be met only if Saudi Arabia was willing to produce oil at the currently imposed production limit of 8.5 MMB/D or more.

Many forecasts suggest that if the major oil consuming countries should be no more successful in their conservation efforts and development of alternative oil and energy sources than they have been to date, world oil import demand would require a Saudi production level of 20 MMB/D—a level far exceeding currently installed producing capacity and which would rapidly deplete even Saudi Arabia's immense oil reserves.[1] With production in other OPEC countries peaking some time in the 1980's, Saudi Arabia's production decision is of even greater consequence. Saudi Arabia may be one of the few producers with spare producing capacity.

Oil production even at current levels generates revenue in quantities that Saudi Arabia cannot utilize effectively domestically, resulting in huge financial surpluses. The amount of oil income will, of course, be affected by oil prices as well, but the implication is that Saudi Arabia has considerable discretionary power vis-a-vis production levels because its domestic needs could be fully met at production levels well below the rate necessary to meet world demand for oil imports. The ability to vary oil production also may affect world oil prices as the Saudis attempted to demonstrate in the aftermath of the December 1976 OPEC meeting.

In addition, to the extent that Saudi production is maintained at high levels, the question of the disposition of the surplus revenue is of fundamental importance to the major industrial powers, the non-oil LDC's and the continued stability and perhaps even viability of the international monetary and the international (public and private) financial systems.

The Saudis have repeatedly stated that their willingness to produce at high levels is in the form of a sacrifice to them—in terms of income lost by producing currently oil that will appreciate in value if left in the ground for future exploitation. The implication is that their continued willingness to make the "sacrifice" depends on the degree to which the industrialized countries recognize that this is a "two-way street," i.e., that they must reciprocate.

The Saudis have repeatedly linked their willingness to produce at levels adequate to meet world oil import demand to Western and

---

[1] Herman Franssen, Congressional Research Service, "Project Interdependence: U.S and World Energy Outlook through 1990" (Washington, D.C.: U.S. Government Printing Office, 1977), pp. 60–61.

Japanese assistance in their domestic industrialization efforts. Moreover, the Saudis have stated that their continued willingness to generate surplus revenue is dependent on the willingness of the industrialized countries to provide investment opportunities guaranteed against the effects of inflation and changes in currency values.

Access to Saudi oil is thus linked to Saudi "absorptive capacity." How much revenue can they effectively utilize, how much surplus will they generate and what will they do with those surplus funds—are all fundamental aspects of the question of access to Saudi oil.

The conventional wisdom has defined absorptive capacity in terms of domestic development plans and the ability of Saudi Arabia to implement them. However, because the vast increase in Saudi oil revenue has had the effect of broadening Saudi conceptions of its international role and influence, a definition of absorptive capacity which relates only to domestic economic goals is probably too restricted.

Domestic development plans and economic and social objectives represent only one determinant of Saudi Arabia's need for oil revenues, albeit a major one. But the ability to use funds is often related to the very size of available funds with needs increasing almost as rapidly as income itself. In this regard it is interesting to note that where the Saudis formerly claimed that their needs could be met at a production level of 3 MMB/D, the necessary production level in 1977 is estimated to be in excess of 5 MMB/D,[2] (which however, is still below the level needed to meet world oil import demand).

A more realistic appraisal of Saudi Arabia's revenue requirements and "absorptive capacity" might include consideration of:

1. Domestic economic plans and goals;
2. Foreign investment opportunities;
3. Foreign policy goals as reflected in Saudi foreign aid; and
4. Military purchases.

It may not be possible to determine an optimal level of Saudi oil production, (this issue is one of the most contentious within Saudi Arabia), but money usually can be spent and a more realistic picture might emerge if all likely opportunities for utilization of revenue are included. It must also be kept in mind that domestic and international political and security objectives will also bear on Saudi decisions regarding oil production levels with at least as much consequence as the economic determinants.

Other essential questions relate to the Saudi development plan and the consequences of its successes and/or failures for Saudi political developments and the kingdom's relations with those foreign countries involved in the plan implementation (including the United States).

The question of access to Saudi Arabia's oil must be directed at the essential question of Saudi oil production levels and the Saudis have linked this to "absorptive capacity" broadly defined.

DOMESTIC ECONOMIC DEVELOPMENT PLANS AND GOALS

The Second Five-Year Development Plan (1976–80) envisages total expenditures exceeding $140 billion (current and capital). The plan's

---

[2] Thomas W. Lippman, "Saudis Call Oil Billions 'Temporary Liquidity,'" the Washington Post, May 23, 1977, Section A, p. 14.

objectives are to: (1) diversify the economy and reduce its overwhelming dependence on oil income for Government revenues (95 percent), foreign exchange earnings (virtually all) and as a share of gross domestic product (87 percent); (2) develop a broad industrial base as a means of diversification: (3) develop human resources; and (4) contribute to the increased standard of living of the population as a whole. These are to be accomplished while maintaining the religious and moral values of Islam and assuring the defense and internal security of the kingdom, the first two plan objectives in order of priority.

Currently perhaps 50 percent of the population is dependent on agricultural and nomadic herding activities while agriculture's contribution to the monetized economy is small and only 10 percent of the total land area is arable. Farming methods are traditional, holdings are small and the lack of distribution facilities means that internal agricultural trade is limited. The main impediment to agricultural development is the scarcity of water so that while only 1 percent of the development plan expenditure is earmarked for agriculture a considerably greater amount is to be devoted to the development of water resources.

Another hindrance to agricultural development is the tendency for Saudis to leave their farms for the cities where they are not qualified for most jobs and unwilling to accept the jobs for which they are qualified. The Government has been active in extending agricultural credit facilities, distribution of new and improved seed and establishing agricultural training centers. Agricultural development is an essential part of the Government's plan to settle the Bedouin. Saudi Arabia imports two-thirds of its food requirements.

Perhaps 40 percent of the labor force is engaged in services including retail trade, construction, and government service. Only 4 percent of the work force is involved in the oil industry. The remainder of the labor force is employed in the industrial sector which is composed of small-scale operations concentrated in three main areas: Textiles and clothing, food processing and furniture, all for the domestic market.[3]

Preliminary studies to determine the existence, extent and commercialization potential of non-oil mineral resources are underway. Saudi Arabia may have commercial reserves of iron ore, copper, gold, chromium, phosphates, zinc, lead, and others.

The Government emphasizes the need for private sector involvement in all aspects of the country's economic development. However, the generally inadequate response of the private sector (although this may now be changing) and the enormous funds available to the Government ($29 billion in 1975–76) have given the Government the preponderent role in economic development. Petromin, the Government petroleum and minerals organization created in 1962, has responsibility for the development of the country's natural resources. It has developed some refining capacity, a fertilizer facility and a small steel operation.

The main thrust of the plan however, involves the Government's huge industrialization projects. The emphasis is on those industries

---

[3] For a fuller discussion of Saudi economic developments to date see, Ramon Knauerhase, "Saudi Arabia's Economy at the Beginning of the 1970's," The Middle East Journal, spring 1974.

in which the country has a comparative advantage; that is, energy and capital intensive industries, or those which offer opportunities for import substitution.[4]

The centerpiece on which many of the other plan projects depends is the gas gathering system designed to utilize 40 to 50 billion cubic meters of gas produced in association with Aramco's oil operations. Aramco is overseeing the project which will feed an expansion of Aramco's natural gas liquids (NGL) facility and a new government facility designed to extract the remaining NGL for transport via a new 1,300 kilometers pipeline to Yanbu on the Red Sea for further processing and export of liquified petroleum gas. Remaining gas will be used to feed a chemical plant, power generating facilities, and a fertilizer plant.

There are also plans for five export refineries, two additional fertilizer plants and seven chemical operations. Industrial developments in non-oil related areas include a steel plant and a possible aluminum plant. Most of these new facilities are to be located on the two giant industrial estates planned for Yanbu on the Red Sea coast and Jubail on the Gulf coast.

In addition, these plans will require: Increased desalination capacity; increased electrical generating capacity; expanded housing construction; and further development of infrastructure.[5]

Gross domestic product is expected to increase at an average annual rate of 10 percent, including 15 percent for non-oil mining and quarrying, 14 percent for non-oil manufacturing, 15 percent for power, construction, wholesale and retail trade, transport and communications, and other services and 4 percent for agriculture.

PROSPECTS

Only rarely in the past have the impediments to Saudi economic growth and development been related to inadequate capital resources.

Rather, hindrances derive from:
  (1) The small size of the population;
  (2) The consequent small size of the domestic market exacerbated by the fact that many people remain outside the monetized economy;
  (3) Poor regional political relations which precluded exports as a means of enlarging the market;
  (4) The small size of the indigenous labor force further circumscribed by lack of training, illiteracy, prohibitions against female participation in the labor force and other social values;
  (5) Wahhabi conservatism;
  (6) Misgivings regarding the social and political consequences of reliance on foreign labor;
  (7) The unwillingness to see economic developments erode the traditional moral basis of the society;
  (8) Inadequate infrastructure;
  (9) Inadequate technological know-how;

---

[4] Dr. Ghazi Algosaibi, "The Strategy of Industrialization in Saudi Arabia," Journal of Energy and Development, (Boulder, Colorado), spring 1977
[5] For a further elaboration on Saudi Arabia's Development Plan see Nicholas Fallon. "Middle East Oil Money and Its Future Expenditure" (London, England: Graham and Trotman, Ltd., 1975), pp. 151–160.

(10) The unwillingness of private investors to commit themselves to long-term projects, preferring quick return, low risk endeavors; and,

(11) Climatic and physical limitations.

In fact, historically Saudi Arabia has been unable to spend the sums budgeted for development.[6] In spite of achievements to date it must be recalled that Saudi Arabia's real economic development planning effort on a systematic basis began only in the early 1960's. The Central Planning Organization was established only in 1965. The system is new and many of the individuals are inexperienced. Moreover, the system is overloaded with projects already underway and a score of new proposals from foreigners eager to share in the petroleum wealth.

Priorities have not been clearly established, the interrelationships between projects are only now becoming clear and the real limitations imposed by inadequate infrastructure have become glaring. Inflation is running perhaps as high as 40 percent and the euphoric atmosphere is hardly consistent with hard work or Wahhabi austerity. Finally, it is becoming obvious that the presumed ability of capital to immediately overcome all the limitations listed above is not valid.

The result has been a stretching out of the plan schedule; the target date of many projects is no longer 1985 but further down the road. This stretching out is consistent with the desires of some in the Government to: (1) stem the inflation rate; (2) restrict the influx of foreign labor; (3) pace change so as to limit disruption to the society and its values; and (4) more nearly match investments with infrastructure developments.

At the same time there has been little slowdown in Saudi expenditures, little is anticipated and some narrowing of the revenue surplus is likely at least for the next few years. The sluggish world economy, the availability of North Sea and North Slope oil and lower oil import demand have resulted in some decline in total oil revenues. Moreover, Saudi Arabia is spending its revenues at a much faster rate than was originally thought possible.[7] Imports have grown rapidly; in 1974 imports were worth $4 billion, by 1975 they had doubled to $8 billion followed by an increase to $12.5 billion in 1976. The estimate for 1977 is $23 billion, excluding military purchases.

In addition while the timetable has slipped, projects generally have not been canceled and the infrastructure investments will need to be adhered to if the industrialization projects are ever to become possible. Delays, infrastructure bottlenecks, high-cost foreign labor and their living requirements—housing, food, et cetera—waste, corruption, and inflation may raise the cost of those projects which are being undertaken. In effect, fewer projects may absorb greater revenue than was originally believed to be the case.

That this may be what is happening is reflected, in part, in the recent rejection by Saudi Arabia of all Western bids for an electrical generating system; the Saudis thought all the bids were enormously inflated and turned to a non-Western contractor—events such as these also fan the Saudi belief that they are being exploited by the industrialized countries seeking petrodollars. The types of projects the

---
[6] Ibid., p. 157.
[7] The Financial Times, "Survey, Saudi Arabia," London, England, Mar. 21, 1977, p. 14.

Saudis have selected, that is, capital intensive, are also the ones which tend to escalate very rapidly in cost.

There are also expenditures which are self-propelling—food, housing and import subsidies, increased salaries for an increasing number of civil servants, tribal subsidies, et cetera—these are difficult to reverse once adopted. Moreover, even with inequitable income distribution, per capita incomes are rising which suggests rising demand for food, housing and consumer products—much of which will require greater imports.

It may be then that Saudi Arabia, which in spite of all its oil wealth remains a less developed country, will continue to require substantial oil revenues for domestic use for many years. The discretionary power to alter oil production levels may be more limited than it was once thought, at least for the next few years.

The sluggishness in worldwide economic recovery and the current oil surplus is consistent with the rescheduling of Saudi Arabia's economic plans and postpones the day when the Saudis have to make the crucial decision concerning production levels, although they must decide now to install necessary additional producing capacity (reportedly they have authorized Aramco to increase producing capacity to 16 MMB/D by 1982,[8] reserving judgment regarding greater, future additions).

Beyond then, when the industrialized countries require additional Saudi production, recurring expenditures may be even larger, economic absorptive capacity may be greater and rising per capita incomes will require imports even beyond those needed for the continued development of the huge, capital intensive industries the Saudis plan. On the revenue side, if the Saudis produce at high levels to keep a lid on prices they will generate greater revenues from larger exports. Alternatively, if the forecast tight oil demand/supply situation materializes, oil prices will increase and again Saudi oil revenues will grow. Moreover, the Saudis will be receiving substantial income from their overseas investments. The Saudi surplus will thus be persistent.

Foreign Investment

With a current surplus of $50–$60 billion and prospects for continued surpluses the question of investment opportunities for these funds becomes critical to continued access to Saudi oil. In addition, to the extent that there is real concern regarding the potential economic, political and social dislocation associated with rapid economic growth and the inflow of foreigners, outward foreign investment might be an attractive alternative to domestic investment. Also, outward foreign investment would provide Saudi Arabia with a non-oil source of income.

The willingness of Saudi Arabia to continue to produce at levels generating a revenue surplus will depend, in part, on the extent to which there are attractive investment opportunities for these funds [9] and greater opportunities for Saudi participation in international monetary and financial institutions.

---

[8] "Middle East Economic Survey," Aug. 29, 1977, volume XX, No. 45 (Cyprus).
[9] Robert Mabro and Elizabeth Monroe, "Arab Wealth from Oil: Problems of Its Investment," International Affairs.

Given the huge funds involved, the United States and European capital markets (particularly London and the Eurocurrency markets) have been the ones to receive the bulk of Saudi funds. This is an important link between Saudi Arabia and the industrialized economies and the international monetary and financial—public and private—systems. When access to Saudi oil is in question the Saudis must consider the impact of their oil policies on the countries in which they have a large and growing economic stake.

Saudi Arabia's international reserves exceed $26 billion, second only to West Germany's, most of which is in the form of Saudi foreign exchange holdings. Although reserves have not been increasing as rapidly in recent years, such large reserve holdings reflect a conservative investment policy.

Most countries prefer not to hold such large reserves because funds held as reserves must be held in liquid form which means that they do not earn the higher rates of interest available for longer-term investments. The Saudis argue that they need liquid funds to pay for projects as they come due. However the preference for liquid funds probably also reflects a lack of trust in Western financial institutions; during the 1973-74 embargo there was talk in the West of freezing Arab funds in the West. The Saudis may want ready access to their funds so they can be moved in anticipation of trouble.

In the industrialized countries on the other hand, it is feared that such funds are subject to manipulation and could be used to disrupt the international monetary system or individual economies. To date there is no indication that these funds have been used in this way. Rather, the Saudis have complained about losses they have suffered as a result of holding sterling.[10] There is no indication to date that Arab governments have used their foreign currency holdings speculatively. Moreover, the industrialized countries do have experience with capital control mechanisms to counter speculative flows.

In addition the Saudi Arabian Monetary Agency (SAMA) may hold an additional $25-$30 billion in foreign assets. A good portion of these take the form of Saudi purchases of government securities, largely in the United States and the United Kingdom. The Saudis may hold as much as $6 billion in U.S. Government securities. The purchase of Government securities reflects also a conservative investment policy in that Government securities, because of the presumed lower degree of risk, have relatively low yields. The bulk of SAMA's funds are believed to be under the control of five American banks.[11]

The foreign assets of the Monetary Agency also include Saudi loans to foreign countries, international development funds and international organizations, including, of course, the loans to the International Monetary Fund's oil facility (over $500 million in 1974 and over $800 million in 1975), and the recently created Witteveen facility (over $1 billion).

Because of the propensity to use brokers or agents, Saudi investments may be understated. Recently the Saudis have been willing to make longer-term investments and it is now believed that funds are

---

[10] Middle East Economic Digest, "Special Report: Saudi Arabia" (London, England), December 1976, p. 27.
[11] Ibid., p. 27.

spread among eight equity and three property portfolios, each under separate management.[12]

More recently the Saudis have demonstrated an interest in triangular investments. This amounts to the combining of Saudi capital with Western—and presumably Japanese—technology and management in a joint venture project in a less developed country.

What has not been provided the Saudis are investment instruments guaranteed against inflation and/or currency changes. Moreover, it is unlikely that such an instrument could be created without inspiring similar demands from every international creditor. To date, the Saudis have not been given a greater voice in the international monetary and financial institutions in which their revenues play such an essential role. It is believed that their initial reluctance to pledge a contribution to the Witteveen facility was related to this continued oversight.

The general animosity which has greeted Arab portfolio or real estate investment is a serious concern. The U.S. Congress was so concerned that in 1974 it demanded that the U.S. Treasury and Commerce Departments prepare studies of foreign portfolio and direct investment in the United States. Given that the United States actively promoted the outward foreign investments of its multinational corporations arguing the numerous beneficial effects of U.S. foreign investment in less developed countries, it is difficult to rationalize the U.S. objection to foreign investment in its own very much larger and more diversified economy. As every industrialized and nonindustrialized country knows, there are means of managing foreign investment's potential negative effects without excluding it. The foreign investment issue may become a sore point in relations between the United States and the country it expects to continue to accumulate surplus funds.

Foreign Aid

Saudi Arabia, along with France, called for the international meeting on North-South issues known as the Conference on International Economic Cooperation (CIEC). The Saudis also linked progress in CIEC and in the North-South dialog generally to Saudi Arabia's continued moderation on the oil price issue. In early 1977, CIEC concluded without much success but the dialog continues in virtually every international forum. Whatever the extent of Saudi Arabia's commitment to LDC's, it will not want to repudiate or appear to repudiate its solidarity with other developing countries.

Moreover, now that it becomes clear that the Saudis can expect to receive unending demands for ever-increasing amounts of foreign aid, it will want the developed countries to assume an increasing share of that burden. This is even more the case in that the international monetary and financial, public and private, systems in which it has a stake appear to be threatened by increasing LDC debt and the possibility of defaults. Whatever the motivation, the Saudis may be insistent on Western and Japanese concessions to the LDC's to get the Saudis off the proverbial hook and the North-South dialog will come to affect oil considerations.

---

[12] Fallon, op. cit., p. 198.

According to the objectives of the Second Development Plan, Saudi Arabia has committed itself to giving 10 percent of its revenues in aid to less developed countries. In the 4-year period 1972–75, the Saudi Ministry of Finance estimates that Saudi Arabia has committed about $11 billion in aid though actual disbursements are probably considerably lower.[13] At least $3.2 billion of bilateral aid took the form of loans.

Saudi aid, as with other donors, is tied to political objectives. In order of priority the frontline Arab States are first. Egypt and Syria have received grants and subsidies and project assistance from the Saudi Arabian Development Fund. Jordan has been a recipient and so has Lebanon. There were reports that the Saudis halted aid to Syria out of disapproval of Syria's action in Lebanon.

In response to Saudi concern regarding the Red Sea region, Saudi Arabia has extended aid to the People's Republic of Yemen, Sudan and Somalia in an effort to reduce Soviet influence in the area. Aid to non-frontline Arab States has been Arabia's second priority. Third come the Islamic countries—Pakistan, Indonesia, Malaysia, et cetera—and finally other "deserving" countries. Aid is also disbursed through the multiplicity of development funds established since the 1973 oil price increases.

Aid is something akin to a bottomless pit. Egypt could probably use all additional funds available but the Saudis are cautious. They probably want to give enough to secure Sadat's position but not so much that Egypt again becomes internationally adventuresome either under Sadat or under some other leader who might replace him in spite of Saudi assistance. Saudi aid is tied closely to Saudi objectives: to assist in the maintenance of moderate regimes and to make radical regimes more moderate.

While there may be room for additional Saudi aid, the Saudis argue that they themselves are a developing country and that the industrialized countries should shoulder more of the responsibility—$2 billion a year on average is already quite substantial. Further increases are likely to be ad hoc responses to immediate developments. It seems unreasonable to expect that foreign aid will absorb much more of Saudi Arabia's surplus revenue.

MILITARY PURCHASES

The claims on Saudi revenues related to military needs will be limited by: (1) The extent to which the Saudis are unwilling to create a military monster which might turn on the regime; (2) the real constraints on military developments related to manpower shortages; and (3) an unwillingness to provoke an Israeli preemptive attack.

On the other hand, Saudi Arabia's military expenditures in recent years have increased substantially because of: (1) the relatively low base from which it proceeds and the need now to replace existing equipment which is quite old; (2) the need not only for equipment but also for training and maintenance services and infrastructure construction; (3) the need to develop simultaneously the military, the police, the internal security forces and the national guard; (4) perceptions of growing potential threats in the Gulf and Red Sea areas; (5) the

---

[13] Financial Times Survey, op cit.

greater arms buildup in Iran and Iraq; (6) some Saudi funding of purchases of military equipment for other Arab States; and (7) the doubling of military salaries.

Given the double-edged sword that an extensive military establishment constitutes, Saudis may prefer to keep American advisers in de facto control of the armed services; Saudi Arabia may not have an interest in the too rapid training of its military. Perhaps the most important factor motivating large military expenditures reflects the desire to involve the United States heavily in Saudi military developments as a guarantee of U.S. willingness to come to Saudi Arabia's defense—the equivalent of the European trip wire—whether the threat is Soviet, Israeli, Iraqi or other.

In 1974–75, the defense allocation was approximately $4 billion; in 1975–76, it was $7.5 billion.[14] In the 1976–77 budget, more than a third or $10 billion is to be expended on equipment, training, maintenance, and construction of military facilities and this figure excludes expenditures on the police force and internal security services.[15]

It is estimated that the United States has from 80 to 90 percent of the market for military goods and services. At the same time, congressional opposition to some arms sales to Saudi Arabia, which the Saudis view as being provoked by the pro-Israeli lobby fearful that Saudi purchases will find their way to the frontline states, may result in greater arms purchases from the United Kingdom and France.

Defense expenditures may continue to take a significant share of the budget for the next several years, before leveling off.

IMPLICATIONS

To return to the initial question as to Saudi Arabia's ability to vary production levels it seems apparent that the Saudis do have a great deal of discretionary power. However, depending on developments in oil prices, that discretion is stabilizing at higher production levels than was expected. The cost of Saudi development projects continues to escalate and import requirements are increasing rapidly. Moreover, at some point in time, it becomes more difficult to dispense with imports; a return to the desert becomes increasingly unpalatable and difficult politically.

Saudi Arabia's trade with the West and Japan is extensive and growing. In terms of markets for Saudi Arabian oil Europe and Japan (60 percent of Saudi exports) are more important than is the United States (20 percent). The EEC and Japan provide 42 percent of Saudi Arabia's total imports; the United States provides 25 percent. The U.S. share of the Saudi import market is actually declining while West Germany and Japan are expanding their shares.

At the same time there is no necessary coincidence between the level of oil production needed to meet Saudi Arabia's domestic requirements and the production level needed to satisfy world oil import demand. The surplus may narrow for a few years but it will persist. It may reappear with a vengeance if the Saudis are called upon to produce 20 MMB/D at substantially increased oil prices.

[14] Fallon. op. cit., p. 157.
[15] Financial Times Survey, op. cit., p. 13.

It is therefore necessary that there be attractive investment opportunities for Saudi surplus funds. Indexation of investment instruments to rates of inflation is unlikely and there is some doubt as to the advisability of creating such instruments. However, a reassessment of U.S. attitudes toward foreign investment in the United States is necessary. It can be argued that Saudi investments in the industrialized countries should be encouraged as a means of giving the Saudis a larger stake in the health and well-being of the industrialized economies. The concept of triangular investments may be an attractive one to the Saudis and should be explored further.

Recent reports suggest that the Saudis may soon have a seat on the International Monetary Fund's Board of Governors. This is a long overdue initiative. In the absence of Saudi participation, the IMF runs the risk of making decisions which are either irrelevant or unenforceable because they require Saudi cooperation and the utilization of Saudi surplus funds.

In addition, further efforts by the industrialized countries on issues of importance in the North-South dialog must be reassessed, not because the Saudis demand it but because it is increasingly clear that the negative consequences of higher oil prices on the non-oil LDC's will affect the industrialized countries. The oil producers will also be affected and perhaps there is room for cooperative efforts in the North-South areas.

With regard to Saudi Arabia's development objectives, the economy envisaged at the end of the plan (whenever that may be) will be one dominated by large, energy intensive, capital intensive industries. An entire range of consumer and capital equipment will need to be imported and those imports may tie Saudi Arabia still closer to the industrialized countries.

In terms of project contracts every industrialized country is represented and the Saudis apparently are eager to involve many countries deeply in their industrialization efforts. Simultaneously, there is a conviction in Saudi Arabia that the country now may be subject to a new form of Western imperialism and exploitation involving high pressure sales tactics and wildly inflated bids with little concern for Saudi Arabia's real needs.

To the extent that the United States-Saudi Joint Economic Commission can dispel these fears and discourage these practices it will serve a very useful purpose in the further development of United States-Saudi relations. The involvement of U.S. companies in Saudi Arabia's development plan is extensive and it is imperative to continued good United States-Saudi relations that these operations be carried out efficiently and effectively.

The continued role of Aramco is significant to access to oil. Apparently agreement has been reached on the transfer of 100 percent ownership of Aramco to Saudi Arabia. The role of the American companies however, will remain important in terms of the technological and managerial services they will continue to perform for the Saudi Arabian Government. In exchange, the companies (Exxon, Socal, Texaco and Mobil), reportedly will have access to 7 MMB/D of Saudi oil production for worldwide distribution. This is quite a significant share of Saudi production. As far as is known there are no Saudi-imposed limitations on the destination of that oil.

Potential areas of disagreement between the United States and Saudi Arabia which may come to affect access to Saudi oil or its terms are: (1) the North-South dialogs; (2) the antiboycott legislation; (3) the Saudi feeling of being cheated; and (4) new U.S. income tax rules which will make it enormously expensive for U.S. personnel to continue to participate in Saudi Arabia's development plans.

If the United States and the industrialized countries fail to provide the Saudis with adequate incentives to produce in quantities needed to satisfy world oil import demand, the United States will have to depend on the leverage the U.S. derives from a U.S. commitment to defend Saudia Arabia and an implied threat to resort to military force if adequate oil supplies are not made available.

III. POLITICAL DEVELOPMENTS

INTRODUCTION

It has already been suggested that the Saudis have a range of choices regarding oil production levels. In contrast, in Iran with its large population and the close relationship between economic growth, oil revenues and political stability, any regime may be constrained in its ability to vary oil policy from one which generates the greatest revenue. The huge increases in oil revenues since 1973 still leave Iran in need of even greater oil income.

In Arabia, the Government has more leeway. This is not to suggest that Saudi Arabia will settle for less income per barrel of oil than Iran receives; it will not. But it is already evident that the issue of Saudi production levels is one of the most contentious within the regime. A change in the policies of the regime or a change in regime may be more consequential to the question of access to Saudi oil than a change in Iran's regime with regard to Iranian oil.

THE POLITICAL SYSTEM

Saudi Arabia is a monarchy and the power of the King is central. As Sheikh of Sheikhs he is the leader of the Bedouin tribes and as imam he is the country's religious leader. He is also Chief of State and Commander in Chief of the Armed Forces. In these latter roles he appoints all ministers, other senior government officials, governors of the provinces and selects all military officers above the rank of colonel. He is assisted by a Royal Cabinet and a Council of Ministers which as of 1958 has some legislative and executive authority but all important laws are issued as royal decrees.

Saudi Arabia's constitutional base is the sharia (Islamic law). The King's powers are neither defined nor limited by law. However, he is committed to uphold historical conceptions as to the quality of leadership and the relationship between the ruler and the ruled. He is limited also by his commitment to serve as defender of the faith and his need to find or achieve a consensus within the royal family. These constraints are real but once their requirements are met the King's decisions are definitive and final.

There are no organized, formal political groups in Saudi Arabia. The royal family is the central political actor and within the family there is a relatively small group, numbering less than 100 people, who actively participate in the political process.

The unity of the family has been an essential bases of political strength. Whatever rivalries and disagreements as to policy exist are submerged before the breaking point in the recognition that disunity could undermine the monarchy. Decisionmaking is therefore, by consensus with the King as final arbiter. Policy is made in royal family councils where individual royal family members by dint of their personal ties with societal groups "represent" these in the decisionmaking process. The workings of the family are secret making a political analysis extremely difficult.

The regime continues to rest on the traditional cooperation among the royal family, the tribes and the religious leaders, reinforced by marriage ties and the distribution of oil wealth. The system functions very much as it always has except that these traditional relationships and the personalism which is an essential feature of Saudi politics may now be filtered through additional institutions; that is, the Council of Ministers.

In recent years technocrats, military officers and businessmen have become more numerous and prominent. However, it is difficult to judge the extent to which these represent separate groups or merely traditional forces in more modern dress, perhaps the sons of the important families and tribes. The influence of these people also is related to their personal relationship with members of the royal family.

Two real strengths of the system relate to the extent to which the royal family permeates every aspect of the society and the degree to which groups are typically related to the royal family rather than to each other.

In the first case, the royal family supplies the Prime Minister (since 1964, the King has served as Prime Minister), the first and second Deputy Prime Ministers and the heads of all the major ministries—Defense, Interior, Foreign Affairs. The National Guard is also headed by a member of the royal family and the governors of the major provinces are either members of the royal family or families closely related to it. Royal family members participate in the armed services, the police, the coast guard and the business community. In addition, the royal princes, who are increasingly better educated, also participate in the technocratic/bureaucratic function.

The second point relates to the closer relationship between influential individuals and the royal family than among the individuals themselves. This pattern of relationships makes it difficult to imagine threats to the regime emanating from a coalition of groups. In addition, the pattern reflects the pivotal role of the House of Saud in maintaining national cohesion; all have an interest in the maintenance of the royal family because of the national unity it provides and the largess it distributes. There may be disagreement on particular issues but there does not appear to be disagreement regarding the system itself or the role of the royal family.

The Royal Family

Most observers agree that the real threat to the regime in the short term may derive from potential rivalries internal to the royal family. The family has demonstrated considerable unity in the past and a recognition that the consequences of disunity do not favor the House of Saud or the monarchy. There have always been clans and factions in the family with groups maneuvering for position; all this generally stops short of the point where it might jeopardize the unity essential to the continuation of the monarchy.

Within the royal family there are important generational differences. Ibn Saud's surviving brothers are important political actors and it is unlikely that major decisions are made without their participation.

Ibn Saud's sons form the nucleus of royal power. Differences within this group stem from different positions on issues as well as competition between clans. The tendency is for Ibn Saud's sons by a single mother to form discrete groups and to develop constituencies within the society.

For example, Crown Prince Fahd with his six full brothers are known as the Sudairi seven. Fahd is next in line for the succession; his brother Sultan is Minister of Defense, Nayef is Minister of Interior and Sulman is Governor of Riyadh. Another brother. Turki is Deputy Minister of Defense. There is some indication that the non-Sudairi members of the royal family are concerned by what appears to be the growing influence of this group.

King Khalid, on the other hand, is from the Jaluwi branch of the royal family. His one full brother, Mohammed is actually his senior but he renounced his claim to the throne. Khalid's ties are with the tribes and the Jaluwis have traditionally controlled the Eastern Province which contains the oil fields.

The divisions within the family have been reflected recently in the apparent inability of the family to agree to a Crown Prince in the event that Fahd assumes the throne. Prince Abdullah who heads the national guard and who is not associated with the Sudairis is a major contender as is Prince Sultan, Minister of Defense, who is a Sudairi.

Khalid apparently represents more traditional tribal and religious forces. In terms of oil policy Khalid may represent those people who are: (1) appalled by the effects of oil wealth and the influx of foreigners on the society; (2) in favor of some retrenchment in the development plan; (3) in favor of lower production levels; and (4) more concerned with Islamic and Arab affairs than world affairs in general. There are those among the technocrats, Hisham Nazir Minister of Planning included, whose advocacy of production levels more consistent with the ability to utilize oil revenue for domestic development coincides with the concerns of these traditional groups.

Fahd is believed to be a "progressive" influence, more attuned to the West than to Arab causes—although no Saudi leader will repudiate either the Arab or Islamic link. Reportedly he, along with Petroleum Minister Yamani, is eager to gain and use the international influence which accrues to Saudi Arabia from maintaining higher oil production levels and a revenue surplus of sufficient size to influence other countries.

The final generational division involves the greater emergence of Ibn Saud's grandsons; that is, the sons of the current Saudi leaders. Their greater involvement as respectable if still junior influences in royal family councils may be of great consequence to Saudi Arabia's political future.[1]

Increasingly better educated—many in American universities—and more technocratically inclined, these younger princes—in their thirties

---
[1] David Long, op. cit., p. 30.

now—represent the link with the emerging technocratic/bureaucratic element. The movement of the royal princes into positions of influence in royal family councils will permit the representation of this group and its need and desires. By modernizing itself the royal family will remain in contact with more modern elements of the society. It is an important link.

POLITICAL DEVELOPMENTS

As far as is generally known there have been few challenges to the regime. In the period of 1958-64 however, the royal family did successfully weather a political crisis involving King Saud, who had succeeded his father in 1953, and his brother Crown Prince Faisal, each supported by different members of the royal family. The basis of the crisis is generally attributed to Saud's mishandling of the country's finances, his extravagances and his challenge to the role of his brothers by placing his sons in positions of influence.

In the course of seeking supporters within the royal family, Saud aligned with Prince Talal who represented the liberal members of the royal family, the so-called free princes. Talal advocated the formation of a partially-elected parliament and limitations on the monarchy. Saud was no more eager to lose his prerogatives to Talal's reforms than to Faisal's influence and Faisal who was serving as Prime Minister rejected Talal's bid for greater power outright. Talal went into exile in Cairo in 1962 where he and three brothers formed the Committee for the Liberation of Saudi Arabia. Apparently Talal repented and returned to Saudi Arabia in 1964 and Saudi Arabia's contact with liberalism passed away unmourned.[2]

In 1962, Faisal assumed control of the government. He issued a program of action [3] which included provisions for: (1) a basic law; (2) uniform regulation of local government; (3) a Ministry of Justice; (4) greater commitment to Islam; (5) social legislation; (6) a coordinated economic development program; and (7) abolition of slavery. In 1964, the royal family with the backing of the ulema (religious scholars) deposed King Saud and named Faisal to be the new King.

Faisal enjoyed considerable authority and prestige. He was an adept and respected ruler. Faisal guided Saudi Arabia into the modern age slowly but steadily apparently recognizing the need for modern adjustments and determined that these should not undermine the Islamic basis of the society to which he was genuinely committed. Economic and social changes were affected; the political system remained as always in spite of changes occurring elsewhere in the Middle East.

In 1975, King Faisal was assassinated. Succession is arranged by agreement of the royal family and confirmed by the ulema. The current King and Prime Minister Khalid Ibn Abd al-Aziz is a son of Ibn Saud and he was installed without difficulty in 1975. Prince Fahd Ibn Abd al-Aziz is Crown Prince and Deputy Prime Minister. To date the succession has been limited to Ibn Saud's sons. King Khalid is approximately 65 years of age; Prince Fahd is about 57.

---

[2] Foreign Area Studies, "Area Handbook for Saudi Arabia," (Washington, D.C.: U.S. Government Printing Office, 1971), pp. 152-157.
[3] Emile A. Nakhleh, "The United States and Saudi Arabia": A policy analysis, (Washington, D.C.: American enterprise institute for public policy research, 1975), pp. 36-37.

IMPLICATIONS

The royal family has demonstrated its capacity for unity. Whatever its internal differences threats to the monarchy and the rule of the House of Saud are not countenanced. The sorts of internal rivalries and maneuverings previously described may be typical and persistant. It is the process of bargaining and balancing which is an essential characteristic of Saudi politics. In terms of oil policy, the need for consensus within the royal family may mean that while the agreed production level will never sink to as low as 5 MMB/D it may also never rise to 20 MMB/D. In terms of access to oil the requirement is for a Saudi regime which is willing to produce oil in quantities sufficient to satisfy world oil import demand.

Unless some external use for the surplus revenue can be found, conservative forces will fear the disrupting effects of oil wealth, the greed, avarice and unwillingness to work engendered by the welfare state and the oil billions and the potential social and political consequences of having large numbers of foreign workers in the country. A balance favoring conservative forces might even see a slow-down or halt in the implementation of the development plan, further increasing the surplus or adding pressure for lower production levels. And a balance favoring conservative forces will see a Saudi Arabia more militant on the Arab-Israeli issue.

A balance favoring more "progressive" forces, however, must still recognize the importance of the religious bases of the society, even as it substitutes government largese as a basis of support for the regime. The rule of the House of Saud is tied to its religious role and no regime can afford to ignore it. Also, any government will recognize the strength of Pan-Arab sentiment.

In the future unity will be subject to additional strain. Oil wealth intensifies the conflicts within the society which are reflected in the royal family, that is tradition versus modernization, Wahhabi austerity versus the requirements of economic development, et cetera. Moreover, if control over the distribution of the oil billions provides a powerful rationale for continued royal family cohesion and gives the regime a means to buy support for the government, it also makes the stakes of political rivalry greater—nothing less than control of the oil wealth and its distribution is the potential prize.

Formal political change has been minimal but apparently there has been little demand for it to date. The link between the younger princes and the new technocrats and the middle class is an important one; it gives the newer groups "representation" in royal family councils and perhaps lessens demands for political change. In 1975, it was announced that a Majlis Shura (consultative assembly) would be established; nothing has been heard of it since.

The greatest dangers are those which are least predictable: that is, a military coup perhaps even inspired by a faction of the royal family. It is not clear how the large involvement of foreigners in military affairs affects the possibility of a coup but it seems reasonable to suppose that the presence of foreigners makes the secrecy necessary for a successful coup more difficult.

Saudi Arabia will not be immune to developments elsewhere in the Middle East. As of now, however, the Saudi regime has probably been strengthened by the fact that: (1) the radical regimes have been discredited; and (2) the political experimentation in Kuwait and Bahrain has been terminated (some say Saudi Arabia was a factor behind the termination). In comparison the Saudi regime may look increasingly good. But the Saudis recognize that their political future will be influenced by developments elsewhere and this, in turn, partially explains Saudi foreign policy goals and objectives.

IV. INTERNATIONAL RELATIONS

INTRODUCTION

If there was ever any doubt that Saudi Arabia's foreign policy objectives would come to influence access to Saudi oil, the 1973–1974 OAPEC oil embargo should have been sufficient to dispel it. A major initiator of the embargo, Saudi Arabia had warned repeatedly that the continuation of the Arab-Israeli conflict and the outbreak of still another Arab-Israeli war would see the invocation of the "oil weapon."

When in October 1973 the United States undertook to resupply Israel, OAPEC instituted an oil production curtailment and a selective embargo directed against those countries (the United States and the Netherlands) which materially or otherwise supported the country with which the OAPEC member countries were at war. Excluded from the embargo were those countries which were judged "friendly" to the Arab cause.

With wider horizons derived from greater involvement in international affairs post-1973, it is possible that additional Saudi foreign policy objectives may come to influence access to Saudi Arabia's oil. It has already been noted that the North-South dialog may be one such factor. But more important the Arab-Israeli conflict remains unresolved and the Saudis have repeatedly stated that "progress" toward a settlement is the cost of continued access to Saudi oil in adequate quantities and at reasonable prices.

POLICY OBJECTIVES AND THE ARAB-ISRAELI CONFLICT

Broadly stated Saudi Arabia's foreign policy is based on three interrelated objectives: (1) to halt or reverse the spread of Soviet influence in the Middle East; (2) to insure political stability and the continuation of "moderate" regimes in the Middle East and the Gulf; and (3) to reach some solution to the Arab-Israeli conflict.

From the Saudi perspective this last is often seen as a precondition to the first two. The Saudis perceive that the Arab-Israeli dispute and U.S. support for Israel have opened the Middle East area to the spread of Soviet influence and the creation of radical regimes closely aligned with the Soviets. Moreover, the future of more moderate regimes is perceived to be seriously threatened by a continuation of the conflict.

No other issue has made it so difficult for the Saudis to maintain a close relationship with the United States. Until 1973, the Saudis had remained aloof from Arab politics (which was largely radical politics) and had played a peripheral role in the Arab-Israeli conflict (some financial aid to the frontline states and some token military assistance). Ties of religion and Arabism make this an extremely difficult position for the Saudis to maintain and the 1967 Arab-Israeli war provoked rioting in Saudi Arabia and calls for more active involvement. Every Arab country has a Palestinian population component to contend with and some resolution of the Palestinian issue is essential to domestic political tranquillity and stability.

A host of factors then converge to commit the Saudis to a resolution of the Arab-Israeli conflict. The Arab cause is one which they cannot repudiate or neglect except with grave internal and external repercussions. In a number of ways over the last few years the Saudis have set the stage for some form of settlement; their prestige and influence in intra-Arab affairs is committed.

It is likely that they will be satisfied with any settlement that meets the requirements of the frontline states and moderate Palestinian forces. But progress is essential; in its absence cooperation with the United States, which is what oil production in quantities necessary to meet the needs of the industrialized countries looks like, will be increasingly difficult and will leave the Saudis exposed to denunciation from radical forces.

While a settlement of the Arab-Israeli conflict may also free Arab radicals for adventures elsewhere (including in Saudi Arabia), on balance the Saudis appear to have concluded that greater threats to their security arise from a continuation of the conflict than from its resolution.

And the Saudis also perceive that only the United States can move Israel in the direction of a settlement and that is what they require. They have not called for a U.S. abandonment of Israel. They see a settlement as being in the interest of all states and U.S. influence is also on the line. The Saudis see that in tandem with the United States they have supported the emergence of moderate (Egypt) or more moderate (Syria) regimes and they do not want to lose that progress.

To date, reports are that they are apparently satisfied with U.S. efforts. In the event of gross disappointment the Saudis do not have to apply the oil weapon again. They merely have to refuse to increase production and perhaps this is all Prince Fahd implies when he says Saudi Arabia will not use the "oil weapon" again. Production limitation would be serious enough when world oil demand recovers.

Radical Regimes

Even in the event of an Arab-Israeli settlement, the United States would be extremely important to Saudi Arabia's security, perhaps even more important; from the Saudis perspective the fundamental threat is from Arab radicalism and subversive organizations. They need not attack Saudi Arabia directly; their success anywhere is an example the Saudis want to spare their population. They can remember back to the late 1950's when Nasser's charisma and perhaps ambitions almost extended to Saudi Arabia. In the event of an Arab-Israeli settlement, Saudi Arabia, oil rich, sparsely populated, militarily unprepared, could be an attractive target and prize.

The Saudis take for granted the U.S. commitment to defend them against direct Soviet incursions; given the importance of Saudi oil such a Soviet move could only be a step in the movement to general war.

The Saudis require the further U.S. commitment to defend them against Arab radicals and they probably have it. Moreover, the Saudis probably assume that U.S. military personnel in Saudi Arabia would participate in Saudi Arabia's defense. Are they wrong? Under the circumstances would the United States refrain from defending the country containing one-quarter of the world's proven oil reserves? Does this involve U.S. defense of the current Saudi regime?

Where Iran may genuinely want to exclude both superpowers from the Gulf, the Saudis may see themselves as being at the mercy of Iraq and Iran if the United States is not involved. Saudi Arabia requires U.S. involvement as a counterweight to these regional powers.

The basis of the United States-Saudi relationship lies in the security area. And it is difficult to imagine that this U.S. commitment, which is nowhere written down, does not involve Saudi undertakings with regard to oil. There is no United States-Iranian Joint Security Commission; there is one for Saudi Arabia.

THE ORGANIZATION OF PETROLEUM EXPORTING COUNTRIES (OPEC)

To date the Saudis have played a moderating role within OPEC. They supported OPEC price freezes, and in December 1976 they split with other OPEC members who instituted an immediate 10-percent price increase to be followed by a 5-percent increase in July 1977. The Saudis opted for a 5-percent price increase with no provision for a July increase. The Saudis also indicated that they were lifting the 8.5 MMB/D production limitation and raising production to 10.5 MMB/D to bring downward pressure on price.

In any event, Saudi production and exports did not increase this high, allegedly because of poor weather conditions in the Gulf. Other factors—that is, oil company stockpiling in anticipation of the December OPEC meeting, good weather in the industrialized countries, slow rates of economic growth—however, did bring downward pressure on oil prices. In addition, the price split was resolved when the Saudis raised prices to the levels prevailing in other OPEC countries while the others agreed to forego the 5-percent July increase.

The Saudis have based their pricing policy on their concern for the state of the Western economies. Slow rates of economic growth apparently convinced the Saudis that further precipitous increases in oil prices would further jeopardize Western economic recovery. The Saudi reluctance to see large oil price increases may be related to a Saudi unwillingness to see Iran accumulate additional revenue to finance even greater arms purchases or to give Iraq additional income. If Saudi Arabia had increased production steadily to the 10.5 MMD/D level, Iranian crude would have been backed out of the market.

But the Saudis have also indicated their unwillingness to continue to stand alone in OPEC councils, although they apparently do not mind demonstrating periodically where the oil power lies. They do not like to appear to be opposing other Arab regimes. They have suggested that the United States should ask its other OPEC-member friends—that is, Iran—to moderate their price positions as well.

The Saudis have opposed production programing and oil price indexation; they will continue to oppose the creation of any automatic mechanism which would diminish their influence in OPEC. Within OPEC, other producers, including Iran, have pointed out the contradiction in Saudi policy which calls for indexation of investment instruments for their surplus funds but opposes indexation of oil prices.

Indications are that indexation of oil prices has lost some of the urgency attached to it by other producers; the suggestion is that the oil demand/supply situation will soon turn tight, and prices will increase naturally and perhaps even at faster rates than the rate of inflation.

In the near term the more important issue may be Saudi Arabia's willingness to continue to unilaterally implement a production programing scheme; that is, to balance Saudi production to world demand so as to maintain prices in the face of the current oil surplus. If the Saudis are no longer willing to do this, other OPEC producers may have to reduce production to maintain prices. The production programing scheme which OPEC never agreed to in the past will be necessary then.

Longer term, prices are expected to increase perhaps regardless of Saudi production decisions; in fact, at much higher prices some other producers may elect to conserve their reserves, depending on Saudi Arabia to increase production to satisfy world needs. In a tight demand/supply situation, Saudi influence in OPEC is more circumscribed while pressure on the Saudis from the industrial countries is intensified.

The Saudis have demonstrated a willingness to assure the free world of the oil supplies it requires at moderate prices. Their ability to do so will be considerably restricted if the industrialized countries do not undertake immediately energy conservation measures and intensified development of alternative oil and energy sources. In addition, the Saudis have other goals including maintaining their influence in OPEC and Arab unity which mitigate against the Saudis permanently precluding all oil price increases, although they may continue to play a moderating role.

General International Affairs

The Saudis have become more active internationally since 1975 although their approach is subtle and discrete. It also depends on the Saudis having available for distribution large amounts of funds.

While the Saudis derive considerable moral influence from their positions as defender of the holy places and the Saudis place great stress on intensifying Islamic ties (particularly when they were isolated from pan-Arab developments and often as the conservative response to Arab unity which until recently had been dominated by the Arab radicals), their current "power" reflects their financial strength. Beyond cash and Islam, the Saudis are short on the ingredients of power.

But to date they have used both to good effect. In the Red Sea area they have attempted to woo Somalia from the Soviets with promises of aid, and they are believed to be considering financing Sudan's military modernization. They have improved relations with the People's Democratic Republic of Yemen.

In the Arab world they have often remained aloof and still do not seek the spotlight. Their influence is to be understood and accepted not paraded. In spite of the ties of Arab unity, Saudi Arabia's Bedouin tradition and the absence of a colonial past distinguishes Saudi Arabs from the others, and the distinction makes the Saudis cautious and sometimes arrogant in their dealings with the other Arab States. There is also the sense that Saudi moderation and tradition have proved out, while the Arab radicals now should see the error of their ways.

In the peninsula, Saudi interest is more direct. The Saud family is related to the ruling houses in Kuwait and Bahrain. The Saudis also assume a position of guardianship over the sheikhdoms which is not always appreciated but which the Saudis expect other countries to recognize. The Saudis apparently resent Iran's direct dealings with the sheikhdoms and believe that Iran should deal with Saudi Arabia vis-a-vis the Gulf States.

While the Saudis and the Iranians are quick to point out the religious bond between them, the Wahhabi Saudis regard the Iranians as heretics. There is also a great deal of Saudi ambivalence regarding Iran's growing military strength.

IMPLICATIONS

Beyond oil wealth, the Saudis have few of the accoutrements of power. With funds to distribute, they can wield influence and they can pay "protection money." But fundamentally their security is tied to the United States, and this must be a factor in Saudi oil calculations. The Saudis assume an American defense commitment; they may assume further that American military personnel in Saudi Arabia will obey Saudi orders in the event of a crisis. The case for the first is strong; the second does not necessarily follow.

While the extent to which the Saudis in reality and action have been a moderating force in OPEC chambers deserves additional research, it is reasonable to assume that a U.S. defense commitment does involve considerations regarding oil. However, if the industrialized countries continue to do so little to improve their domestic energy situations, a tight demand/supply situation will rob the Saudis of influence on oil prices. If the Arab-Israeli conflict continues without progress toward some form of settlement, the Saudis will be less able to produce in quantities necessary to satisfy world oil import demand at reasonable prices even if this is their sincerest intent.

PART IV.—IRAN

I. HISTORICAL RELATIONS WITH THE WEST

INTRODUCTION

Throughout history Iran's strategic location between "east" and "west" inevitably involved it with both. Dating from the beginning of the 19th century however, Iranian developments were dominated by Britain and Russia—their rivalry as well as their cooperation. The history of Persian weakness and the inability of Iran to maintain real (as opposed to ostensible), independence in the face of these two powers continues to influence Iranian foreign and domestic policies and also goes some distance toward explaining Iran's policies toward other major powers, including the United States. One need refer back no further than 1941–46, to be reminded of more distant expisodes which saw Persia wracked by the interference of these two foreign powers and the memory continues to be influential.

BRITAIN AND RUSSIA

British interest in Persia derived from Britain's position in India and increasing concern that Napoleon meant to strike England indirectly by attacking India via Persia.[1] Once this apparent threat to the Empire was recognized, British interest was guaranteed. From that time forward Britain resolved that no other major power establish a dominant position in Persia, placing Britain squarely in conflict with long-standing Russian ambitions in the area.

In the first half of the 19th century British policy encouraged Iran to oppose Russian expansionism without, however, offering substantial material assistance. Britain was tied down in the Napoleonic wars and the vicissitudes of the European situation sometimes found England and Russia allied, sometimes in opposition. British support for Iran was dependent on the more general state of Russo-British relations which was determined by European developments. With only sporadic and half-hearted British support the Shah had little alternative but to succumb to Russian demands in geographic areas where Persian control was nominal in any event.[2]

Russian interest in Persia reflected the desire to obtain a Gulf port through Iran. From the early 1800's, Iran and Russia were sporadically at war. In 1813, the Russians took advantage of their temporary alliance with Britain to press their claims while Britain was unlikely to oppose them. By the terms of the Treaty of Gulistan, Iran ceded a vast expanse of northern territory to the Russians.[3]

Note: Until 1935, the country was called Persia. While Iran is generally used now, both are used interchangeably William Haas, *Iran*, (New York: Columbia University Press, 1946), p. 30.
[1] William Haas, *Iran* (New York Columbia University Press, 1946).
[2] Yahya Armajani, *Iran*, (Englewood Cliffs, N.J · Prentice Hall, Inc., 1972), p. 107.
[3] George Lenczowski, *The Middle East in World Affairs*, (Ithaca, N.Y.: Cornell University Press, 1962), pp. 29–31.

(67)

At the conclusion of the second war with Russia (1825–28) Iran signed the Treaty of Turkamanchai. By the terms of the treaty the infamous capitulations were instituted, giving Russia extraterritorial jurisdiction over Russian subjects in Iran. In addition, Iran ceded territory up to the Aras River and granted Russia considerable economic privileges in Persia.

The 1860's marked another period of Russian advance in Central Asia.[4] Defeated in the Crimean War and frustrated in Europe, Russian expansion in the area to the east of the Caspian Sea not only compensated for the failures in Europe but also reflected the traditional Russian concern with the security of its borders, which now appeared threatened by Britain's northward advance from India. Moreover, to the extent that Russian activity kept Britain occupied in Asia, Russian pressure might divert, or at least divide, British attention from Europe.[5]

At about the same time, Britain expanded its influence in the Gulf and in 1856, the British defeated Persian attempts to assert control of a portion of Afghanistan. By the middle of the century Iran had surrendered an extensive array of powers normally exercised by a sovereign government within its own territory. Iranian independence was nominal and extracted by playing the powers against each other.

The very weakness of the central government was both a cause and a result of foreign intervention in Iranian affairs. The weakness of the Qajar dynasty (1779–1925), reflected in the prevailing anarchy in the countryside and sporadic tribal rebellion, facilitated foreign intervention as did the mounting level of foreign debt accumulated to finance the Iranian Government and the royal household. However, foreign intervention often precipitated tribal unrest and the inability of the government to secure Iran against foreign encroachments further undermined the authority and legitimacy of the regime.

By 1885, the Anglo-Russian rivalry shifted from questions of territorial expansion to competition for political and economic influence in Persia. Because the goal of each power was largely the negative one of denying advantages to the other, Persia's interests often were not of primary concern.[6] Economic developments often were paralyzed when one or the other great power vetoed activities which might confer an advantage on its rival and the costs of great power rivalry were multiplied by the unwillingness of Britain and Russia to allow third parties to participate in Iranian economic developments.

The competition for concessions bred corruption and political dissent as Persians saw their resources sold to foreigners through bribery and individual and royal avarice.[7] Iran's economic position continued to deteriorate, further weakening the regime and increasing its dependence on its Russian and British creditors; by 1906. the Iranian Government was in debt to Russia to the extent of 7½ million pounds sterling.

In 1906, the reaction against corruption, poor and arbitrary administration, financial chaos, political and social anarchy and foreign

---
[4] Armajani. op cit., p 109.
[5] Vartan Gregorian. *The Emergence of Modern Afghanistan*, (Stanford, Calif.: Stanford University Press 1969). p 110.
[6] See Parker Thomas Moon, *Imperialism and World Politics*, (Toronto: The Macmillan Co . 1926)
[7] Nikki R. Keddie. *Religion and Rebellion in Iran: The Iranian Tobacco Protest, 1891–1892*, (London: Frank Cass and Co., Ltd., 1966), p. 3.

intervention resulted in a successful, nationalist effort to force the Shah to accept a constitution. However, assisted by the Russians, the Shah attempted to rescind the constitution; the nationalists, supported by the British, successfully resisted but Persian politics took on the characteristics of civil war.

In large part, Britain and Russia were acting out their more fundamental rivalry in Europe on the safer Persian stage. When it was a question of the multinational empires of the Hapsburgs or the Ottomans, British and Russian policies diverged. When however, a third power rose to challenge the European status quo—that is, Napoleon in the 1800's, Imperial Germany in the opening years of the 20th century and Hitler's Germany in the late 1930's—Britain and Russia resolved their differences to act in concert. If the Persian position was poor under conditions of great power rivalry it was even worse under conditions of great power cooperation.

In 1907, Russia and Britain resolved their European difficulties in response to the rise of Imperial Germany. The Anglo-Russian Convention of the same year resolved their differences in Persia as well; the de facto division of Persia became de jure as Russia assumed control of the north, Britain the south and a third, neutral area separating the spheres of influence was established.

The Persians then turned to Germany in hopes of finding there the "third power" necessary to oppose Russian and British ambitions in Persia. Given these growing ties with Germany, the outbreak of World War I saw Persian neutrality violated as Russian forces moved into the northern provinces and the British secured the south and the oilfields. Neutral Iran became a battlefield.

In 1919, with the Russians preoccupied with the aftermath of the Bolshevik Revolution and the strategic importance of Persian oil clearly demonstrated during the war, the British proposed an Anglo-Iranian treaty which would have had the effect of turning Iran into a British protectorate.[8] Not only did the Majlis refuse to ratify it, but shortly afterward a treaty was signed by Persia and the new Soviet Government.

According to the treaty of February 26, 1921, the Soviet Government renounced all past treaties concluded between the Tsarist Government and Persia. Weak and eager to secure its southern flank and to distinguish itself from Tsarist imperialism, the Soviet regime: (1) renounced all extra-territorial privileges; (2) agreed to the withdrawal of all Soviet troops; (3) abandoned all concessions (except the one for the Caspian fisheries); and (4) canceled all debts.

The Soviets also agreed to withdraw their support for secessionist forces in Gilan and Mazandaran. However, the treaty did stipulate that the Soviet Union could intervene in Iran should a third party seek to use Persian territory as a base of operations against the Soviet Union.

The interwar years, under the nationalist leadership of Reza Shah Pahlavi witnessed Iran's growing freedom from foreign intervention in Iranian internal affairs. The British oil concession was canceled in 1933 until the company (owned, in part, by the British Government),

---

[8] Haas, op. cit., p. 139.

agreed to terms more favorable to Iran.⁹ In spite of the Soviet regime's desire to present itself as a nonimperialist power, the Saadabad Pact (1937) was anti-Soviet in intent and suggested that the signatories (Iran, Turkey, Afghanistan, and Iraq) were not totally convinced that the change in ideology meant a change in Russian ambitions. Relations with Germany were intensified.

In his desire to modernize Iran, Reza Shah often relied on foreign advisers (as indeed had previous regimes). In addition, increasing numbers of Persians were sent abroad for an education. At the same time Iranian policy sought to involve as many different foreign countries as possible in Iranian developments so that no one of them would gain a dominant place.

In 1941, as if nothing had occurred in the intervening years, the British and the Russians composed their differences to meet the challenge of Hitler's Germany and again intervened in Iran, forcing the Shah to abdicate and again dividing the country between them. In January 1942, the de facto occupation of Iran was acknowledged in the British-Soviet-Iranian Tripartite Treaty. The foreign powers pledged their respect for the territorial integrity and independence of Iran and agreed that all foreign troops were to be evacuated within 6 months of the conclusion of the war.

The Tehran Declaration (1943) again pledged Britain, the Soviet Union and now the United States to recognize and respect the territorial integrity and independence of Iran. British and American forces were withdrawn in 1945-46 in accordance with the provisions of the Tripartite Treaty.

However, the continued Soviet occupation of northern Iran, Soviet support for the secessionist movements in Azerbaijan and Kurdistan, support for the Communist-dominated Tudeh party and Soviet demands for an oil concession in northern Iran, suggested a different Soviet intent. Moreover, the failure of the Soviets to evacuate their troops demonstrated to Iranians that there was little difference between Soviet and Tsarist intentions in the area.

In April 1946, under Russian pressure, the Iranian Government agreed to: (1) establish a joint Soviet-Iranian company for the exploration of oil reserves in the north; and (2) include Communists in the government. With this agreement, U.S. diplomatic support and some assistance from the U.N. Soviet troops were withdrawn in May 1946, 2 months after the deadline.¹⁰ The Iranians reneged on the Soviet agreement, Tudeh ministers were dismissed from the government and the Majlis refused to ratify the oil agreement.

At least three lessons emerged from this experience with foreign intervention. The first relates to Soviet designs on Iran and the Gulf. By an accident of geography Iran is positioned south of a huge and powerful neighbor with historic interests in the area. Changes in Soviet ideology and regime do nothing to dilute that interest. The means and methods may change but continued Soviet interest in developments on its southern flank is assured. While cooperation with

---

⁹ Leonard Mosley, *Power Play: Oil in the Middle East*, (Baltimore, Maryland: Penguin Books, 1973). p. 91
¹⁰ George Lenczowski, op. cit., p. 195, and Tareq Y. Ismael ed., *The Middle East in World Politics A Study in Contemporary International Relations*, (Syracuse New York. Syracuse University Press, 1974), p. 96.

the U.S.S.R. is not precluded, an awareness of Soviet ambitions remains in the background and introduces caution in Iranian-Soviet affairs.[11] The 1,250-mile border with the U.S.S.R. is a constant consideration in Iranian Policy.

Therefore, Iran perceives a need to secure the involvement of another power, preferably one with no territorial or other ambitions regarding Iran, but with a similar interest in opposing the Soviet Union. The British were never entirely satisfactory in this role. British policy vacillated between support for a strong, independent Iran as a buffer state between Russia and India, or a Persia divided into spheres of influence or a Persia administered by Russia and Britain. Moreover, the Britsh often made common cause with Russia when their more important European interests dictated such a policy. In fact with Britain's conflicting ideas as to Iran's future and British monopolization of Iran's oilfields, the need was for a "third power" to oppose Russian and British ambitions in Iran.

The second lesson derived from foreign intervention in Iranian affairs relates to the desirability of balancing foreign interests so as to: (1) secure Iran's independence; (2) avoid excessive dependence on any one country; and (3) extract maximum freedom of maneuver for Iran.

Germany's defeat in World War II eliminated that country as a potential balancer. Increasingly it was only the United States which could play the role and in spite of American reluctance, Iran attempted to involve the United States in Iranian affairs. From the Iranian viewpoint there is a natural coincidence of interest between Iran and the United States vis-a-vis the Soviet Union.

There was a new recognition that Iran's very weakness provided foreign powers the opportunity to intervene in Iranian affairs. Moreover, experience suggested that in the future Iran must be prepared to take up some of the responsibilities of self-defense; other countries had a number of interests other than Iran and could not always be relied on to come to Iran's assistance if other, more important interests dictated a different course of action.

The third lesson derived from the experience of Anglo-Russian rivalry then relates to the need for Iran to be politically, economically, and militarily strong if Iran is to avoid being again a playground for foreign powers. Only such an Iran would be of interest to the United States (although such an Iran might be a more attractive target for the Soviets). A strong Iran also would be better able to defend itself, not necessarily militarily, but from the newer forms of Soviet penetration; for example, subversion.

THE UNITED STATES

Apart from some early, minor contact between American trading ships, U.S. contact with Iran dates from the early 19th century and the activities of American missionaries.

From 1829, American Protestant missionaries were involved in building and managing schools and hospitals as well proselytizing.[12]

---

[11] His Imperial Majesty Mohammed Reza Shah Pahlavi, *Mission for My Country*, (London. Hutchinson and Co., Ltd., 1961), p. 119.
[12] See Elgin Groseclose, "Introduction to Iran," (New York: Oxford University Press, 1947).

Only in 1883 were diplomatic relations initiated between Iran and the United States and the United States maintained a legation in Iran until it was upgraded to embassy status during World War II.

Private Americans did however, play a substantial role in Persia. In 1911, the Iranians hired Morgan Shuster to serve as treasurer-general. His assignment was to bring order to Persia's chaotic finances.[13] The Russians, with British acquiescence, sabotaged the mission and compelled the Persian Government to expel Shuster before he could make any progress.[14]

In the early 1920's, Iran approached the U.S. State Department. Describing Persia's "open door" policy, Iran indicated its interest in encouraging American private investment in Iran, particularly in a northern oil concession, and requested a financial adviser. Under the direction of Arthur C. Millspaugh a financial mission did begin operations in Iran in 1922.[15] The mission, however, was private and paid for by the Iranian Government.

In addition, the Standard Oil Co. of New Jersey (now Exxon) and the Sinclair Oil Co. did, separately, indicate interest in a northern oil concession provided that transportation of the oil either through the Gulf or Russia could be arranged. The Russians and the British refused to provide transit rights and neither company pursued the matter further.[16]

Increased American involvement in Iran dates from World War II. Iran, occupied by British and Soviet forces, served as the transit route through which allied supplies were transported to the Soviet Union. Initial American involvement was related to military requirements. U.S. missions were assigned the tasks of: (1) administering lend-lease and the grant military assistance program; (2) reorganizing the gendarmarie; and (3) reorganizing the quartermaster and supply departments of the Iranian army. American involvement at this stage, and for some time in the future was directed at internal security not external defense.

In addition, by the terms of the Tehran declaration, the United States and United Kingdom, and the Soviet Union undertook to provide Iran with economic assistance.[17] A new financial mission, again headed by Arthur C. Millspaugh was dispatched to Iran in 1943.[18] Other American advisers were active in the areas of agriculture and food, health, police, and education. In 1946, an American, Max Thornburg, assisted in the preparation of Iran's first development plan. These missions were financed by the Iranian Government.

In spite of this greater U.S. involvement in Iranian military and economic affairs, American policy continued to reflect the belief that the Middle East was Britain's responsibility. Only when Britain's weakness and desire for retrenchment became clear and the Soviet Union's ambitions became evident did the need for a larger American role in international affairs become apparent.

---

[13] Maurice Harari, "Government and Politics of the Middle East," (Englewood Cliffs, N.J.: Prentice Hall, 1962), p. 39.
[14] See W. M. Shuster, "The Strangling of Persia." (New York: Century, 1912).
[15] Arthur C. Millspaugh, "The American Task in Persia," (New York: ARNO Press, 1973 reprint of 1923 edition).
[16] Armajani, op. cit., p. 145.
[17] For text see Haas, op. cit, pp. 256–7.
[18] Arthur C. Millspaugh, "Americans in Persia," (Washington: Brookings, 1946).

The Truman doctrine (1947), was the first manifestation of greater U.S. international involvement and it enveloped Greece and Turkey in a U.S. protective umbrella as well as giving them access to Marshall Plan aid and sophisticated military equipment. No such initiatives were contemplated vis-a-vis Iran and Iran argued, with justification, that it was at least as exposed to the Soviet Union as Turkey and, therefore, as valuable an ally.

The Shah visited the United States in 1949 and requested aid. He was told that aid was dependent on Iran's implementation of domestic political and economic reform which the Shah attempted.[19] There was then considerable disappointment and embrassment when American aid was not forthcoming on anything like the scale envisaged. U.S. assistance in the period 1949-52 totaled only $33 million.[20]

In face of a precarious financial position and the unwillingness of the Anglo-Iranian Oil Co. to provide Iran a greater share of oil profits, Iran nationalized the company in 1951. Related to the nationalization. Iran was in the throes of xenophobic nationalism and political instability which threatened the continuation of the monarchy. Disturbed by apparent Communist gains in Iranian politics, the United States played a major role in settling the oil dispute and restoring the Shah and the monarchy.[21]

As a result of the settlement the U.S. role in Iran expanded to include the participation of American companies in the newly formed oil consortium which replaced Anglo-Iranian. The consortium consisted of Anglo-Iranian's successor, BP (40 percent), Royal-Dutch Shell (14 percent), Compagnie Francaise des Petroles (8 percent), and Standard Oil of California, Exxon, Texaco, Mobil, Gulf, and a group of American independents held the remaining shares.

Additional American military assistance bolstered the strength and effectiveness of the military and intelligence services, both of which became important sources of support for the Shah. In the period 1953-57, U.S. aid to Iran totaled $500 million, of which economic aid was $367 million and military aid $133.[22] There has been a conviction, sometimes verbalized by the Shah, that because U.S. financial assistance had not been forthcoming in adequate quantities immediately following World War II, the political crisis of 1951-54 was made more likely.[23]

In 1955, Iran joined the American-sponsored Baghdad Pact, only to find that the United States was not going to join (although it did participate in some Pact activities). The Eisenhower doctrine (1957), extending the U.S. security commitment to the Middle East, addressed the Arab countries, still excluding Iran. It hardly seemed an appropriate reward for Iran's participation in the Baghdad Pact, which every Arab country, except Iraq, refused to join. (After the 1958 coup Iraq withdrew and the pact was renamed the Central Treaty Organization, Cento.) In 1959, the United States signed a bilateral security agreement with Iran, allaying some fears regarding the U.S. defense commitment to Iran.

---

[19] His Imperial Majesty Mohammed Reza Shah Pahlavi. op. cit., pp. 88-89.
[20] Marvin Zonis, "The Political Elite of Iran," (Princeton, N.J.: Princeton University Press, 1971), p. 108.
[21] Ibid., p. 89.
[22] Ibid., p. 108.
[23] Lenczowski, op. cit., pp. 202-225.

In 1956, perhaps to demonstrate that there were alternatives to U.S. assistance and perhaps in response to domestic political pressure, the Shah began mending fences with the U.S.S.R. The early 1960's witnessed further attempts at improving relations between the two countries. Improved relations with the Soviet Union are not precluded but there are limits on the relationship and improved relations often have the appearance of a carefully orchestrated affair of civility between two parties who continue to oppose each other and know that they oppose each other in spite of such tactical maneuvers.[24]

At the same time, the United States is the only viable "balancer" available, while experience has demonstrated that such a power is often unreliable and sometimes a Trojan horse and no substitute for Iranian economic, political, and military strength.

---

[24] His Imperial Majesty Reza Shah Pahlavi, op. cit., pp. 122–24.

II. CURRENT FOREIGN RELATIONS: THE IRANIAN AND UNITED STATES PERSPECTIVE

INTRODUCTION

It is commonly asserted by Iranians that the United States does not recognize or act upon its true national interests. The implication is that if the United States did recognize its own interests it would see that these coincided with Iran's. A corollary is that the United States does not appreciate adequately Iran's contribution to the defense of these common interests.

Moreover, these interests are at least as essential to the United States as the interests engaged in Western Europe, and Iran therefore must be accorded treatment equivalent to that accorded Western Europe. There is an Iranian perception that in the past, the United States has made its assistance conditional on internal reforms in Iran which demonstrated America's complete misunderstanding of the Iranian situation and assumed a relationship other than one of equality between the United States and Iran which is no longer acceptable.

Given the Nixon doctrine, the assumed unwillingness of the United States to become deeply involved far from its shores and the associated U.S. policy of relying on regional powers in support of U.S. interests, it is incomprehensible to many Iranians that the U.S. Congress is apprehensive about arming Iran sufficiently to play the role which U.S. policy itself dictates.

Related to the conviction that Iran must be sufficiently strong economically, politically, and militarily to defend Iran's interests is the conviction that the United States is other than a totally reliable ally (witness the 1965 and 1972 Indo-Pakistani wars, Angola, Vietnam) and that, therefore, Iran must be prepared to defend its interests as it defines them.

Because there is no reason to doubt the sincerity of Iranians who claim to be neither pro-American nor pro-Soviet, but pro-Iranian the only test of the value and durability of the United States-Iranian relationship may be the degree to which United States and Iranian international objectives coincide.

SOVIET UNION

The overriding objective of Iran's Soviet policy is to protect Iranian territorial integrity and sovereignty from Russian incursion. Within this central goal, Iran's position vis-a-vis the Soviet Union is a complex balance among three objectives: (1) the desire to refrain from provoking the Soviet Union; (2) the desire to improve relations with the Soviets to the extent possible and consistent with Iranian independence in order to gain whatever advantages might accrue from such a position; and (3) the desire to forestall the extension of Soviet influence in the geographic region of particular interest to Iran (i.e., the Gulf, Indian Ocean, Middle East and the Indian subcontinent as well as northern Iran).

While improved Iranian-Soviet relations are possible and often serve Iranian and Soviet purposes (the border with China necessitates a secure border with Iran), on another level the countries remain in direct opposition. The 1,250 mile border with the U.S.S.R. is lightly guarded on both sides but it is a powerful influence in Iranian foreign policy formulation.

Historical Soviet ambitions in the Gulf, Soviet support of subversive activities in Iran and elsewhere, apparent Soviet support for Baluchi and Pathan separatists, Soviet ideological hostility to the traditional, monarchical regimes with which Iran identifies, the increasing Soviet naval presence in the Indian Ocean, the Red Sea and the Gulf and Soviet influence in Iran's neighbor states (Afghanistan and Iraq), are all disquieting to Iran. In addition, Iranian fears are multiplied to the extent that recent forecasts [1] suggest that the Soviet Union may require substantial oil imports which could come only from the Middle East, with uncertain implications for future Soviet policy in the area.

Trade with the Eastern bloc countries was more important when Iran did not have sufficient hard currency earnings to finance purchases in the West and Japan; the East Europeans were more amenable to the barter trade Iran then favored. At the same time, Iran's non-oil exports to the Eastern bloc countries remain important as these goods are often not of sufficient quality to sell in the West or are excluded by Western and/or Japanese trade policies.

Fear of the Soviet Union is often the first point made by Iranians in seeking to justify their arms buildup. In the unlikely event of a direct Soviet attack on Iran, Iran's military capability is designed to forestall an easy Soviet victory. Vis-a-vis the Soviets, the military requirement is that Iran should be able to hold out long enough to permit a response from the world community and particularly the United States.

In addition, in justifying the arms buildup, Iranians compare their forces to the arms that the Soviets have supplied Iran's western neighbor, Iraq. Iranians, conscious of the long border with the Soviets, watchful of Soviet positions in Iraq and Afghanistan (but not apparently in India) and apprehensive of possible encirclement by pro-Soviet forces are at a loss as to the questioning of their military requirements by the United States. From an Iranian perspective the Soviet threats to Iran's security are real and numerous and the validity of the proposition that what threatens Iran threatens also the continuous flow of oil from the Gulf to consuming centers is self-evident.

The United States

The basic premise of Iranian foreign policy is that U.S. involvement in Iran effectively counterbalances Soviet power. With the superpowers in stalemate, Iran accepts responsibility for countering indirect Soviet aggression and subversive activities. Thus while the role

---

[1] Central Intelligency Agency, "The International Energy Situation: Outlook to 1985," April 1977.

envisaged for the United States is crucial (and it is unlikely that Iran perceives that any other power could play this role), it is generally described as a passive one of deterrence and stalemate within which Iran has a great deal of freedom of maneuver.

At the same time, Iran's policy is not one of neutralism but one of "positive nationalism". In effect Iran is as closely alined with the West and particularly the United States as is consistent with: (1) the objective of not provoking the Russians; and (2) the extreme sensitivity of Iranians to any appearance of foreign intervention in Iranian internal affairs.

Positive nationalism has required substantial arms purchases, mainly, but not exclusively, from the United States, and military/security/intelligence cooperation with the United States both of which have been straining the limits of Soviet tolerance.

While Iran accepts the need for a U.S. presence in areas where the Soviet Union is active, in general, Iran favors the exclusion of the superpowers from the Indian Ocean/Gulf/Red Sea area. Any greater U.S. involvement might invite the greater Soviet involvement that Iran wants to avoid. Any lesser U.S. involvement, it is suggested, might encourage Soviet adventurism.

Western Europe and Japan

In the Iranian schema, Western Europe and Japan are important as: (1) counterweights to the United States, and (2) economic actors. Moreover, to the extent that Iran is of importance to U.S. allies as a secure source of oil supplies, it is of enhanced interest to the United States.

Relations with the industrialized countries other than the United States are cultivated. Some arms purchases originate in Europe and Iran repeats that in the event the United States does not sell it the military equipment it believes necessary, alternative sources could be found easily in Western Europe.

In the economic area relations between Iran and Western Europe and Japan are more extensive than United States-Iranian relations.

In 1976, Japan received 20 percent—almost 1 MMB/D—of its total crude oil imports from Iran; Western Europe received 16 percent—or over 2 MMB/D—of its crude oil imports from this source. The United States received only 6 percent—500,000 B/D—of its crude imports from Iran. From the Iranian perspective the European and Japanese markets absorbed over 60 percent of Iranian oil production while the U.S. market accounted for only 6 percent.

With regard to Iran's non-oil exports. in 1974–75, the EC absorbed 30 percent, Japan 5 percent and the United States 8 percent. On the Iranian import side—excluding military sales—the EC provided 30 percent, Japan 15 percent and the United States 20 percent. Japanese exports to Iran have been the fastest growing, while of the European countries, Germany is most important.[2] Until 1972, Iran had a nonpreferential trade agreement with the EC and new negotiations with the EC are in progress.

---

[2] Iranian-American Economic Survey, 1976/2535, (New York: Manhattan Publishing Co., October 1976), pp. 69–71.

Foreign investments in Iran from Europe and Japan are substantial with recent Japanese investments in petrochemicals heading the list. Out of 183 private investors operating in Iran, 60 percent are from Western Europe and Japan.[3] In awarding government contracts Iran apparently has distributed them widely among all the industrialized countries.

Iranian outward foreign investment has been more welcome in Europe than in the United States or Japan. The Iranian purchase of 700,000 shares in British Petroleum[4] and investment in Eurodif and Krupps have been agreed. In contrast negotiations for Iranian equity participation in Pan Am and Occidental Petroleum and the planned purchase of some of Ashland Oil's marketing facilities in the United States all failed to result in positive action, for a variety of reasons, som economic and some political.

For technology, contractors, imports of goods and services and trade opportunities, Iran is apparently convinced of the value of the West—including the United States and Japan. Eighty-nine percent of Iran's exports and 86 percent of Iran's imports originated in these countries.[5] Furthermore, the extension of financial assistance to the United Kingdom (where, however, actual payment of the Iranian loan appeared to be related, or the Iranians tried to relate it, to Britain's willingness to arrange barter deals for Iranian-United Kingdom trade) and Italy reflects the belief that Iran's interests are tied to the West—as well as a little comeuppance from an LDC extending aid to two countries of the industrialized West.

With regard to European and Japanese roles in the geographic areas of concern to Iran, the emphasis is on the economic contribution these countries might make to the economic development of the LDC's. The assumption appears to be that to the extent that Western Europe and Japan contribute to the development efforts in LDC's, the long-term opportunities for political stability and invulnerability to subversive activities are enhanced—in spite of the recognition that in the short-term development may be destabilizing, requiring perhaps Iranian intervention or involvement. Europe and Japan can contribute and because they have no superpower ambitions, they can contribute more effectively and in a politically acceptable way.

THE GULF

Beyond Soviet threats to Iranian security, Iranians point to the Gulf and the need to defend it as the second justification for their arms build-up—the two problems are, of course, related. In addition, Iranians argue that deefnse of the Gulf, through which almost 75 percent of the oil in world trade must pass on its way to consuming countries, is at least as important to the United States as it is to Iran.

Iranian interests in the Gulf are historical, economic, strategic and political.[6] Iranian interest in the Gulf was rekindled when, in 1958, the Iraqi monarchy was overthrown and replaced by a radical regime. This initial threat to the monarchical principle and traditional regimes

---
[3] Jacqz, op. cit., p 379.
[4] Journal of Commerce, July 14, 1977.
[5] Ibid , pp 361–362
[6] See Rouhollah K K. Ramazani. "The Persian Gulf: Iran's Role," (Charlottesville, Va.: University Press of Virginia, 1972).

in which Iran has an obvious interest, was exacerbated when in the 1960s Egypt's President Nasser engaged first in a propaganda battle against traditional; that is, "reactionary" regimes in the Arab world and Iran and later in an actual military battle against the religio-royalist forces in Yemen. Preservation of the status quo in the Gulf is associated with the health of the monarchical system and traditional rule in Iran.

Further urging and allowing a more active role for Iran was the 1968 announcement of Britain's intention to withdraw from the Gulf by 1971. Iran was concerned that the potential power vacuum should not invite in extra-regional powers. The Gulf states should assume responsibility for the security of the Gulf and Iran is prepared to do so either in concert with other Gulf states—who have little real military capability—as Iran proposed in 1970 or alone—witness the Iranian seizure of Abu Musa and the two Tumbs in the strategic Straits of Hormuz, possibly with British acquiescence.

Iran's economic interests in the Gulf are, of course, extensive and still growing. Iran's major oil producing fields are located in southwest Iran near the Gulf coast; the Abadan refinery is connected with a Gulf port and Kharg Island, the world's largest oil export terminal, is located in the Gulf.

Iran also has interests in offshore oil. fisheries and intra-Gulf trade. Approximately 1 million Iranians live on the Arab side of the Gulf and there is a sizable Arab community on the Iranian side. Iranian banks, businesses, schools, and hospitals are established in the Arab States of the Gulf.

The economic and strategic importance of the Gulf will be enhanced as planned economic developments increase the economic importance of southern Iran.[7] Inadequate inland water supplies necessitate the location of many industrialization projects on the Gulf coast: nuclear power generating plants, three steel mills processing 70 percent of Iran's planned steel output in the 1980's and petrochemical facilities will be located on the Gulf. There are also plans for desalinization operations on the Gulf and the Gulf of Oman. Several military facilities are slated for the Gulf as well.

From the Iranian perspective even a cursory glance at the Gulf littoral states is sufficient to justify Iran's position as defender of the Gulf. Iraq is alined with the Soviet Union, allows Soviet naval forces to use its Umm Qasr port facilities at the northern end of the Gulf, houses several, subversive, revolutionary groups and has irredentist claims against Kuwait.

With regard to internal developments. Kuwait's experiment in parliamentarianism is uncertain as is Bahrain's political experimentation. Iran has had little confidence in the ability of the Saudi royal family to make the social changes and modernization efforts Iran believes to be vital to Saudi stability. The United Arab Emirates consists of a union of tiny sheikdoms who continue to harbor territorial and dynastic rivalries. In Oman. Iran participated. at the invitation of the Omani ruler. in military operations against rebel forces operating from Dhofar and allegedly supported by the Soviets and/or

---

[7] See Amir Taheri. "Policies of Iran in the Persian Gulf Region," in Abbas Amirie. ed., *The Persian Gulf and Indian Ocean in International Politics,* (Tehran : Institute for International Political and Economic Studies, 1975).

the People's Republic of China. In effect not only are the Arab States unlikely to be able to defend the Gulf, the potential for internal instability and susceptibility to subversion is great.

Since the late 1960's some contentious issues in the Gulf have been resolved. In 1968, Iran and Saudi Arabia resolved territorial disputes regarding two Gulf islands and agreed to divide the related seabed resources. Additional continental shelf agreements were reached between Iran and Abu Dhabi, Bahrain, Dubai, Oman and Qatar.

In 1970, Iran submitted its claim to Bahrain to the United Nations and accepted the results of a U.N. report concluding that Bahrein preferred independence to association with Iran.

In 1975, Iran and Iraq signed an agreement settling all their differences including those relating to the Kurds and the Shatt al-Arab at the head of the Gulf. Relations with Iraq apparently continue to improve and Iran is attempting to woo Iraq from its dependence on the Soviet Union.

Iran has greater confidence in the new Saudi regime of King Khalid and Crown Prince Fahd to insure domestic stability in Arabia and the United Arab Emirates has successfully weathered a constitutional crisis in favor of strengthening the federation's institutions.

Iran has repeatedly called for greater cooperation among the Gulf littoral states, including but not exclusively a Gulf defense pact. Intra-Arab politics, Iran's quarrel with Iraq and Iran's relations with Israel were apparently inhibiting factors.

Similarly, Iranian proposals for a Saudi-Iranian defense link have not resulted in agreement. In spite of common interests in oil, religion (although Iranians describe common religious ties as a unifying factor in Saudi-Iranian relations, the Saudis are Sunni Muslims of the orthodox Wahhabi sect and Iranians are Shi'i Muslims and the sects do conflict) and support of traditional regimes, there remains a great deal of suspicion of non-Arab Iran's intentions by some of the Gulf states on the Arab side. The recent Iranian emphasis has been on cooperation and conciliation in the Gulf but the seizure of the two Gulf islands demonstrates a willingness to use force when vital national interests are involved that gives rise to concern in the states on the opposite side of the Gulf.

From an Iranian viewpoint, Iran's defense of the Gulf is consistent with the interests of the United States and those of the littoral states and fills a much-needed role which the other countries cannot. While it is unlikely that any Arab country could openly support this proposition, it is not a completely far-fetched one. Barring any Iranian territorial ambitions, tacit acquiescence, very private cooperation and public protest might be expected from the Arab side of the Gulf in the event of an Iranian intervention. At a minimum there is ambivalence toward Iran's continued military build-up from the other side of the Gulf but not the total opposition often described in the Western press.

ELSEWHERE

With the 1973–74 increases in oil prices, Iran's international horizons expanded and armed with oil money, Iran's international influence increased as well. Iran's role to date has been one of conciliator and balancer, attempting to counteract the polarization of areas by too close an association with either superpower.

Iran has supported U.N. resolutions calling for the creation of an Indian Ocean peace zone and nuclear weapons free zones in the Middle East, Africa, and South Asia. On a visit to the Far East in 1974, the Shah proposed a South Asian security system and a common market. Iran's trade ties with Australia, New Zealand, India, Pakisan, Indonesia, the Philippines and North and South Korea are to be expanded. In addition, skilled workers were recruited in South Korea, the Philippines, India and Pakistan.

In 1972, Iran reaffirmed its commitment to the territorial integrity and independence of Pakistan. The internal political situation and threats of further dismemberment of Pakistan are of concern to Iran. Pakistani secessionists are opposed as any success might give encouragement to their coethnics on the Iranian side of the border. Iran has played an active role in conciliating Pakistan, India and Afghanistan.

At the same time Iran recognizes India as a major regional factor and has been active in forging closer ties; the joint Iranian-Indian Madras refinery and Iran's pledge to supply it with crude oil is one indication and Iranian aid to India—$133 million in 1974—is another.

Other large Iranian aid recipients include the Arab frontline states. Egypt was to be a major recipient with lesser sums allocated for Syria and Jordan. Improved relations with Egypt and Syria are motivated in part to ween them from a return of Soviet influence in one case and continued Soviet influence in the other.

It is difficult to say much regarding Iranian-Israeli relations beyond noting their existence. The Iranian pledge to supply Israel with oil was a major contribution to the conclusion of the Sinai disengagement accord. But Iranian-Israeli relations are conducted far from the public view. To the extent that both countries see threats to themselves in Arab radicalism, cooperation between the two countries may be extensive, perhaps particularly on the level of cooperation between the two intelligence services.

A continuation of the Arab-Israeli conflict, to the extent that it results in Saudi production limitations or Saudi acquiescence in oil price increases is not necessarily inimical to Iranian oil interests. And to the extent that the Arab-Israel conflict keeps the Arab countries; i.e., Iraq, occupied elsewhere a continuation of the conflict may be consistent with Iranian interests.

However, to the extent that the Iranians see a continuation of the Arab-Israeli conflict as destabilizing to the moderate Arab regimes and an invitaion to Soviet penetration in the Middle East, Iran may favor some form of Arab-Israeli settlement. In addition, without a settlement, continue Iranian-Israeli ties are at least one factor but probably not the major one, making a Gulf defense pact or a Saudi-Iranian defense pact unlikely.

With the disappearance of the financial surplus Iran's international relations may become more selective. The basic thrust however, is to limit superpower involvement in geographic areas of interest to Iran or, if this proves impossible, to balance superpower involvement in such a way that stalemate ensues. Within stalemate, Iran will encourage and participate in regional cooperation efforts where Iran's relative power position is enhanced by the exclusion of the superpowers. Iran's position vis-a-vis the superpowers will be enhanced in turn by its regional influence.

Nuclear Option

Iran plans to vastly expand its nuclear power electrical generating capacity in the next decade. France and Germany are already committed to building two nuclear reactors each in Iran. There is the possibility that Iran may purchase as many as eight reactors from the United States although it has been difficult to reach agreement on safeguards. With substantial oil, gas, and coal resources the emphasis on nuclear power reflects a desire to husband oil and gas resources for export. There is probably also a matter of the prestige associated with having nuclear facilities.

Iran has signed and ratified the Nuclear Non-Proliferation Treaty. The Shah has stated that Iran does not intend to develop nuclear weapons, although he cautions that such a decision would be re-examined if other regional actors should develop nuclear weapons capability. Also, the Shah links his willingness to forego nuclear weapons to the ability of Iran to purchase, primarily from the United States, all the conventional weapons he deems necessary to Iran's defense.

Iran's nuclear reactors will be subject to the safeguard provisions of the International Atomic Energy Agency and such additional safeguard, as may be required by nuclear-technology exporting countries. Iran also has supported U.N. resolutions calling for the creation of nuclear weapons free zones in the Middle East, Africa, and south Asia. Most recently (April 1977), the United States and Iran agreed to exchange technical information and to cooperate in the area of nuclear safety.

At the same time, Iran is participating in European uranium enrichment facilities (Eurodif and Coredif) and perhaps in a similar operation in South Africa. The participation in uranium enrichment facilities may reflect the desire to avoid dependence on foreign sources of enriched uranium fuel for the reactors to be built in Iran. Iran has also purchased an interest in the West German heavy engineering and nuclear equipment company, Deutsche Babcock and Wilcox A.G.

Iran apparently has found a way around U.S. concern regarding the proliferation potential of national enrichment facilities by investing in enrichment operations outside Iran—perhaps not an entirely objectionable way in light of U.S. proposals for multilateral nuclear facilities to reduce the danger of nuclear weapons proliferation. Given the vast expansion planned in nuclear power generating facilities, Iran's nuclear ambitions deserve close watching.

Military Purchases

Iran argues its needs for the considerable arms purchases it is currently contracting on several grounds. The first is the Soviet threat either directly or through one of the Soviet Union's regional client states. In part, the objective is to deter; that is, to discourage adventurism.

Second, is the need for Iran to defend the Gulf and the oil supply routes in the face of the inability of the countries on the Arab side of the Gulf to do so and their vulnerability to subversive activities.

Third, the Iranians argue that their arms purchases are deceptively large because they include training and maintenance contracts and contracts for infrastructure development.

Fourth, arms purchases appear to be great but in reality they were anticipated and are cyclical; that is, Iran's current equipment is more than 15 years old and is due for replacement. New arms are replacements not necessarily additions to existing equipment.

Implications—The U.S. Perspective

1. Given Iran's strategic location there can be no doubt that the United States has an interest in Iran's security. The U.S. interest in the continuous flow of oil through the Gulf is identical to the stated interest of the current regime and implies a commitment to Iran's defense.

2. The United States has an interest in Iran's economic, political, and military strength. Such strength will deny the Soviets the ability to confront the United States with a fait accompli and, therefore, discourages Soviet adventurism.

3. The question of defense of a particular regime is more difficult; it is not certain that all changes or any change in Iran's regime necessarily means a change in Iran's need for continuous oil revenues and therefore, continuous flows of oil through the Gulf.

4. The United States has an interest in the defense of the Gulf. This interest must remain demonstrably clear and the warning must be an ever-present consideration in Soviet policy formulation that threats to the continuous flow of oil through the Gulf would so endanger the Western and Japanese economies as to be grounds for general war.

5. The degree to which Iranian and United States interests in the Gulf continue to coincide depends on the extent to which Iran continues to exercise restraint in playing the role of defender of the Gulf. Only under the conditions of Iranian restraint can the United States continue to rely on the broader coincident of Iranian and U.S. interests and remain physically distant from the area.

6. The United States is not committed to resupply Iran with military equipment or parts in the event of an Iranian military action which does not serve U.S. interests. Other countries have not felt necessarily compelled to do so in other situations in other countries. United States arms supplies are tied to the pursuit of U.S. interests. Iranian protestation to the contrary, the United States has every right to ask, "what for?" The presence of a large number of American personnel raises questions regarding their involvement in internal troubles or external defense. Here too the United States must remain free to withdraw its personnel. The presence of U.S. personnel and the presumed inability of Iranians to utilize all the recent arms purchases could give the U.S. leverage over any Iranian intention that runs contrary to U.S. interest.

7. In spite of the general coincidence of interest between the United States and Iran, Iran has additional interests; that is, defense of the traditional regimes, Saudi actions as to price and production levels, which are not necessarily identical to the U.S. interests in the area. There may be different conceptions as to threats and the means of defending the Gulf.

8. It is necessary, however, to be clear as to what Iran's role may require because under certain circumstances that role may be controversial and extremely sensitive. First, it is the U.S. interest which defends against the Soviets. Iran's strength is a necessary adjunct.

Second, the many intra-Gulf issues and conflicts may not threaten the flow of oil, but may provide opportunities for Russian intervention. Iran's role as conciliator is, therefore, important.

Third, the most serious threats may emanate from internal changes in Gulf states. Not all changes in regime will threaten the flow of oil but they may, or they may threaten the status quo which in Iran's view would threaten its own regime and hence threaten the security of the Gulf. These are threats to which Iran may be capable of responding. Intervention in the internal affairs of other countries is difficult and, even when accepted by other countries as necessary in a particular instance, will be unacceptable as a general principle. Iran's strength, however, can have deterrent value. But if Iran is called upon to intervene in the internal affairs of any Gulf state, it must be recognized in advance by the United States that this is the role for which Iran is being primed and blame cannot be assigned for Iran's carrying out an implied assignment.

9. There are hints of Iranian nuclear cooperation with Israel, South Africa and/or Pakistan which cannot be substantiated but which merit attention.

10. Historically the Persian Empire occupied a far larger geographic area than does present-day Iran. When Persian leaders were strong their ambitions were great. Weakness could have similar effects as foreign successes are called upon to compensate for domestic failures. In addition, as Iran's oil reserves peak and decline, across the Gulf will be Saudi Arabia with plentiful oil reserves, enormous wealth and little to spend it on in terms of native population as seen from Iran.

III. ECONOMIC DEVELOPMENTS

INTRODUCTION

The interest in Iran's economic development stems from a number of sources. There is relatively little differentiation between the economic and political systems. In fact, it is probably inappropriate to speak about autonomous economic and political systems. Rather there are economic and social development goals about which there can be no disagreement (and hence no politics) and to which all national energies are directed. In effect, no real political development is possible until the country and the people are "ready" and ready implies substantial economic and social development and change.

Economic developments will suggest sources of pressure and demands on the government in the form of newly-emerging social forces and their relative strengths. And economic developments will indicate the resources available to the government to meet those demands. The use of the economy for essentially political objectives; that is, providing Iranians with a stake in the continuation of the system, building a sense of national commitment, preempting potential discontent, all emphasize the importance of sustained economic growth. And the close relationship between the economic and political system means that economic development and growth are now factors in maintaining the legitimacy of the government.

In addition, Iranian economic developments will influence the nature of Iran's relations with other countries. This is not economic determinism but merely recognition that Iran's economic goals and ambitions will be important factors influencing Iranian foreign policy and the ability of Iran to play an international role.

United States concern with Iran's economic developments relates to:
    1. The impact of economic and social change on Iran's political development and change;
    2. The implications of economic developments for Iran's oil policy; and
    3. The relationship between economic change and Iran's foreign policy formulation and capabilities.

STRUCTURE OF THE ECONOMY AND DEVELOPMENT GOALS

In 1977, Iran's economy and future economic development remain heavily dependent on oil and oil revenues. Before the 1973-74 price increases oil accounted for 55 percent of government revenue and 76 percent of foreign exchange receipts (1972-73); after the price increases oil provided 84 percent of government revenue and 89 percent of foreign exchange earnings. In 1974-75, oil accounted for 45 percent of gross national product (GNP).[1] In absolute terms oil revenues increased from $4 billion in 1973 to $18 billion in 1974.

Oil has been the driving force in Iranian economic development. Oil revenues have financed Iran's development plans as well as a portion of current expenditures. Indeed revenues from the oil sector have permitted the government to undertake ambitious development plans by: (1) financing necessary imports; (2) providing a painless source of savings making heavy taxation and other restraints on consumption unnecessary; and (3) stimulating private investment as the government injects oil revenues into the economy via government spending and credit facilities.

Oil money has allowed Iran to pursue economic growth and social welfare objectives simultaneously. Finally, the oil sector, through backward, but particularly forward linkages has provided an impetus to further industrialization and economic development.

Since the early 1960's, Iran has experienced rapid rates of economic growth. In the decade 1962-73, real GNP increased at an average annual rate of approximately 10 percent. Following the oil price increases of 1973-74, Iranian GNP grew at exceptionally high rates (72 percent in 1974-75) and while much of this growth was attributable to the increased value of oil production, other sectors of the economy have also registered impressive rates of growth. In 1975, GNP (at market prices) was estimated at $49 billion.

The agricultural sector has been the laggard in the system; in the period 1963-67 the agricultural growth rate was 2.5 percent a year, accelerating to approximately 4 percent a year in the 1968-72 period. Rapid population growth and increasing per capita incomes, however, resulted in increases in demand for agricultural products of 10 to 12 percent a year. Iran currently imports 30 percent of its food requirements.

The world food crisis and Iran's growing dependence on food imports resulted in increased government attention to the agricultural sector as part of a comprehensive rural development scheme in the Fifth Plan period (1973-78). In 1973-76, there was some improvement in agricultural performance but the growth rate (6 percent) still fell below plan targets and the growth rate believed necessary to achieve the government's goal of 80 percent food self-sufficiency by the mid-1980's.

The sector continues to suffer from unfavorable climatic conditions, scarcity of water and irrigation facilities, rural illiteracy, antiquated methods, fragmented landholdings, inadequate credit and extension services, and lack of distribution and marketing facilities.[2] Agriculture employs about 40 percent of the labor force but contributes only 15 percent of non-oil GNP (23 percent in 1971-72).

The industrial sector, including manufacturing and mining, construction and electric power, on the other hand, has experienced rapid rates of growth. Real growth in this sector averaged 13 percent a year in the 1971-76 period. The average annual rate of growth in manufacturing and mining exceeded 13 percent in the period 1960-76, and power grew at a rate of 25 percent a year during the same period.[3] In

---

[1] Jahangir Amuzegar, *Iran: An Economic Profile*, (Washington, D.C.: The Middle East Institute, 1977), p. 63
[2] See the Financial Times, "Financial Times Survey Iran," (London, July 25, 1977).
[3] Amuzegar, op. cit., p. 63.

part, these numbers reflect the relatively low base figures on which growth is calculated, but the direction of economic change is clear. The industrial sector accounted for 30 percent of non-oil GNP in 1975-76 (up from 26 percent in 1971-72) and employed over 30 percent of the labor force. A great deal of private industrial activity, however, is still concentrated in small workshops; textiles and food processing continue to head the list of industrial employment. Fifty percent of manufacturing production is nondurable consumer goods.

Finally, the service sector, including transportation, communications, banking and insurance, public and private services, et cetera, grew rapidly and in 1975-76 contributed approximately 55 percent of non-oil GNP. Thirty percent of the work force was engaged in the service sector.

Iran's development objective is nothing less than the transformation of the economy from one dependent on oil to one in which industry sustains continued economic advance. Diversification of the economy away from dependence on oil is the primary long-term aim. As oil revenues and production level off and begin to decline, Iran's industry will absorb increasing amounts of oil while supplying manufactured goods for export to compensate for oil's declining contribution to foreign exchange earnings. In the immediate term, the Government seeks to capture the value added in the petroleum sector through refining and petrochemicals projects.

The Nature of the Task

The Iranian population in the mid-1970's is estimated at 35 million people, growing at an annual rate of approximately 3 percent. While this figure is not large in comparison to Iran's total land area (essentially equivalent to the land area of Western Europe, including Great Britain), it is substantial in terms of available agricultural land and water resources. Moreover, even with a vigorous, Government-supported family planning effort and greater female participation in the economy, the population could total 55 million by the early 1990's.[4]

The age distribution of the population is skewed with some 45 percent of the population 15 years of age and younger, and 3 percent of the population 65 years old and older.[5] With further declines in infant mortality and the death rate, this population distribution is expected to remain characteristic of Iran through the 1980's. As a result, the size of the economically dependent population is large and will remain substantial through the 1980's.

The literacy rate in 1975-76 was estimated at 38 percent of the population aged 10 years and older; the male literacy rate (48 percent) is higher than the female rate (27 percent) and the urban literacy rate exceeds the rural rate. By the end of the fifth development plan (1977-78), the overall literacy rate is forecast to be 44 percent of the population (55 percent of the males, 33 percent of the females).[6] The greatest gains have been made among youngsters in the 10 to 19 years of age group which augurs well for the future labor force; adult illiteracy, however, remains a current problem.

[4] See Kayhan Research Associates, "Iran Yearbook 1977/2535." Teheran, pp. 45-46.
[5] See Jane Jacqz, ed., "Iran: Past, Present and Future," (New York: Aspen Institute for Humanistic Studies, 1976), p. 44.
[6] Iran Yearbook, op. cit., p. 43.

School enrollment at all levels has been increasing rapidly, but coverage remains less than total. In addition, because children often are needed as a source of family income, the dropout rate is high—40 percent at the primary level and 70 percent at the secondary level.[7] Primary education is free and compulsory, and the minimum working age has been increased; enforcement, however, remains difficult.

The need for a better educated labor force for further economic progress is recognized. There is also increasing concern that the school system be more responsive to the needs of the economy with a growing emphasis on vocational training. University enrollments stood at 135,000 in 1974–75 as compared to 75,000 in 1970–71.[8] Approximately 25,000 Iranians are enrolled in universities in the West.

Compounding the lack of trained teachers, the wide geographical dispersion of the population makes the extension of government services difficult. While there is an increasing trend toward urbanization (perhaps 47 percent of the population in 1977–78), the definition of urban is crucial. If "urban" refers to those localities having a population of 10,000 people or more, the urban population is only 36 percent of the total. Forty-five percent of the population lives in areas with less than 1,000 residents, and it is estimated that 4.5 million people live in 48.000 villages with a population under 250.[9] The magnitude of the task of nationally integrating these people is understandably immense.

While the proportion of the population in rural areas is declining, the absolute number of rural inhabitants continues to increase. Only increasing standards of living in rural areas will stem the rural-to-urban drift which results in the severe straining of facilities in the few large urban areas; Tehran, Isfahan, Ahvaz. and Mashad grow at an annual rate of approximately 5 percent.

Geographic dispersion is exacerbated by the great ethnic and linguistic diversity characteristic of Iran. Perhaps only 60 percent of the population speaks Farsi, the official language. Farsi-speaking Persians in villages and towns throughout the central plateau are surrounded by Kurds, Arabs, Lurs, Bakhtiari, Qashqai. Khameseh, Shahsavan, Baluchis, and the Turki-speaking tribes of the north.[10]

In the past when the central government was weak, these groups often seized the opportunity to free themselves from Iranian authority. One of Reza Shah's first acts after building a strong military force was the subduing and disarming of the tribes. A great deal of government attention is focused on efforts to keep these people satisfied with their position in Iran—now using economic and social welfare incentives.

With regard to religion there is greater homogeneity: 98 percent of the population is Muslim, and 90 percent of these are Shi'ites (the Kurds and Arabs, however, are Sunni Muslims). Although the trend has been toward the increasing secularization of the society, religion remains an important factor, and the legitimacy of the monarchy is related to the role of the monarch as defender of the faith. There are

---

[7] Ibid., pp. 399–405.
[8] Ibid., p 405.
[9] Jacqz. op cit , p 164
[10] Groseclose, op cit

also religious minorities in Iran including Jews, Armenian Christians, Zoroastrians, and Bahais.

Population size, its age distribution, geographic dispersion and ethnic diversity suggest the magnitude of the development task in Iran. This is multiplied by increasing per capita incomes; per capita income in 1975-76 was estimated to be about $1,300 compared to $800 a year in 1973.[11] Income distribution also may have potential political consequences. While it appears likely that the standard of living of most Iranians is higher than it was 10 years ago, the relative gain of various socio-economic groups and geographic regions may vary widely.[12] Government policy has been concerned with more equitable income distribution and the extension of government services designed to raise the standard of living (if not necessarily the income) of the poorer segments of population. High rates of inflation further distort income distribution and most seriously affect the urban middle and working classes.

Changes in the work force have resulted in this emergence of urban working and middle classes. Of an estimated 10 million people in the labor force in 1974-75, approximately 34 percent were still engaged in agriculture (43 percent in 1970), while the absolute number of people in agriculture actually declined somewhat and fell below industrial employment for the first time in 1975-76.

At the same time, 34 percent of the labor force (3.1 million people) were engaged in industry and industrial employment was double the figure of a decade earlier. Thirty percent (3 million people) were engaged in the service sector.[13] Given the government's development plans, these trends are expected to continue.

To date unemployment per se has not presented much of a problem and under the current development plan a labor shortage in certain categories necesitated the use of foreign contract labor and resulted in increased pressure for greater female participation. Rather, problems of employment relate to agricultural underemployment, a shortage of skilled, managerial and professional labor and a mismatch between available labor and the types of employment opportunities.

The picture that emerges is one of a developing country which is dependent on sustained levels of economic growth to: (1) meet the needs of a rapidly growing, increasingly better educated, youthful population enjoying rising expectations and rising per capita incomes; (2) wield together a large and diverse country; (3) balance to some acceptable degree economic gains from region to region as well as from economic class to class; (4) provide higher standards of living generally without necessitating the politically difficult step of deliberate income redistribution; (5) enlist the positive support and commitment of university-trained technocrats so essential to further economic advance; (6) provide employment opportunities for surplus agricultural employees and the increasing number of school graduates; and (7) create additional and alternative bases of political support among various segments of the population. Under the circumstances high levels of economic activity are not a nationalistic whim but a political necessity.

[11] Jacqz, op cit., p. 60.
[12] Amuzegar, op cit., p. 257
[13] Ibid., pp. 15-19.

Political Uses of Economic Development

LAND REFORM

The importance of sustained economic development to the political system is enhanced by: (1) the use of economic tools for political ends; and (2) the use of economic mechanisms to pre-empt the types of problems that have characterized other developing countries.

The most obvious use of economic policies to affect political developments was the land reform program. Control of villages and tenants, including the ability to: (1) redistribute land at will as a reward or a punishment; (2) extend credit; and (3) supply necessary agricultural inputs, gave landowners considerable influence over the tenants and hence, political power.

In 1951, the Shah began the land reform program with the distribution of crown lands. If the distribution of crown lands was intended to serve as an example to the large landowners to do the same, the subsequent 1955 land reform enacted by a Majlis dominated by them suggested that the landowners were willing to distribute state lands as a substitute and not as a prelude to their own liquidation. The 1960 law which did deal with privately-held land was so weak as to be ineffective.

In 1962, taking advantage of the suspension of the Majlis, the 1960 land reform law was amended by cabinet decree and approved by the Council of Ministers; this law is regarded as the original land reform act.[14] According to its provisions, limits were set on the amount of land which could be owned by a single individual. With the completion of the third phase of the land reform program in 1971–72, it was estimated that 70 percent of all the tenants in the country had received ownership of the lands they cultivated.[15]

The political intent of land reform is clear; the program was to break the political power base of the large landowning families, the tribes and the leaders of the Islamic clergy and it was successful in this regard. The more difficult task was to substitute the government as a focus of support and loyalty. This involved providing services previously supplied by the landlord, which continues to prove difficult given the wide geographic dispersion of the villages. In addition, land reform created a landless rural proletariat of over 2 million people.

But more important is the continued uncertainty regarding the future structure of agricultural landholding. Once the government turned its attention to the economics of the agricultural sector, the need to consolidate landholdings became apparent. The government encouraged the formation of rural cooperatives, farm corporations and agri-business and in 1975 a bill aimed at comprehensive rural development was enacted. In effect there is some tension between the twin goals of enlisting farmer support for the government and the assumed requirements for agricultural development. There is further tension between the goals of raising farm production and keeping agricultural prices low.

---

[14] See Ismail Ajami, "Land Reform and Modernization of the Farming Structure in Iran," in *The Social Sciences and Problems of Development*, edited by Khodadad Farmanfarmaian, (Princeton, N.J., Princeton University Press, 1976), pp. 189–206.
[15] Ibid., pp. 194–97.

The medium-sized farms which produce 70 percent of the marketable crop have been squeezed between higher prices for agricultural inputs (seed, fertilizer, machinery) and government efforts to keep food prices to consumers low. The medium-sized farmer remains dependent, in the absence of any alternative, on the distribution facilities of the bazaaris and the middlemen who further reduce the income accruing to the farmer. The small-holder may leave his land fallow as he takes a higher-paid job in industry.

The Fifth Plan devoted some $6 billion (current and capital) to agriculture and it was anticipated that $1.9 billion would be invested by the private sector. The fundamental failure of the agri-businesses and state-run farm corporations has resulted in greater emphasis on the private farmer in the Sixth Plan.

Amid increasing evidence that the private farmer responds favorably to appropriate economic incentives combined with a renewed interest in a traditional system of farm consolidation (boneh system) and emphasis on comprehensive rural development schemes, policy may be redirected and more responsive to the needs of the medium-sized farmer.

The government continues to court these farmer-proprietors to: (1) mobilize them for the agricultural development needed to reduce food imports; (2) provide a growing market for expanding industrial production; (3) constitute a conservative basis of political support; (4) fortify the group against subversion by giving them a stake in the system; and (5) halt the rural-to-urban drift and the potential radicalization of the migrants.

PROFIT SHARING AND SHARE PARTICIPATION

In 1963, the Shah enunciated his program of economic and social reform known as the Revolution of the Shah and the People or the White Revolution. In it the Shah called for industrial profit sharing to: (1) prevent the radicalization of labor; (2) give workers a direct stake in the efficient operation of the company; (3) mobilize workers to the tasks of development; (4) distribute income more equitably throughout the system; and (5) avoid the labor-management problems existing in other countries.[16]

Another principle of the White Revolution involved the sale of government corporations to the public. Land reform was to be financed from the proceeds of the sale of government companies and the landowners were provided with investment opportunities for the compensation they had received for the sale of their land.

In 1975, to widen the industrial ownership structure, to create a stock market in Tehran and to give more Iranians a direct stake in the continued health and well-being of the Iranian economy, the Shah announced the share participation plan, subsequently enacted by the Majlis.

Ninety-nine percent of the shares of public corporations (excluding heavy industry) were to be sold to workers, farmers, and eventually the general public. In addition, 320 private companies were required to sell off 49 percent of their shares in the same way. The government

---

[16] Iran Yearbook, op. cit., p. 352 or Amuzegar, op. cit., pp. 225–227.

has created credit facilities specifically for workers and farmers interested in purchasing shares. By July 1977, 151 companies had offered 20 percent of their shares for sale and the entire program is to be completed by March 1978, although there apparently has been some relaxation in the timetable. In 1977, 72,235 industrial employees and 125,745 farmers had become shareholders.[17]

THE WHITE REVOLUTION

The enunciation of the principles of the White Revolution coincided with a reemergence of political activity by the opposition National Front in the early 1960's. The White Revolution program was designed to demonstrate the regime's progressive character. If land reform and profit sharing were aimed at enlisting the support of farmers and laborers respectively, the White Revolution was aimed at preempting the political opposition and enlisting the support of the technocrats and the university-educated in an enormous and revolutionary development effort.

PRIVATE INVESTORS

While the reforms were aimed at cultivating the support of newly emerging social forces (the farmer/proprietors, the industrial working class and the university-educated, urban middle class), an uneasy and ambivalent relationship prevails between the government and private investors many of whom are the old landowners dressed in modern entrepreneurial garb.

On the one hand government policy has been to encourage private investment through tax incentives, tariff protection, low-interest loans and provision of infrastructure. Every development plan envisaged major contributions to investment from the private sector. The government's sphere was to be heavy industry and key sectors (oil and gas, petrochemicals, copper, steel, etc.) while the private sector was to be active in all other areas.

However, private investment is appreciated only when it coincides with the government's economic plans and objectives. There has been considerable government disappointment in the continued propensity of private investment to flow into construction (but not into the low-income housing which is so much needed), high and rapid return projects and overseas investments. Moreover, the share participation plan not only provided investors with new sources of capital but also diluted the power derived from control of enterprises. The profit sharing plan also can be viewed as an attempt by the government to prevent the solidification of a new basis of political power for the former landlords now turned industrialists. The Iranian system is based on an unwillingness to countenance the formation of sources of power outside government control.

Most recently the government has instituted price controls to slow inflation and has cracked down on people suspected of hoarding and profiteering, particularly the middle-men. In the anti-inflation campaign some major industrialists were arrested. Also, given the need to control inflation and the government's increasing concern that Iranian industry be internationally competitive (to substitute for oil exports) tariff protection will be less readily available in the future.

---

[17] Financial Times, op. cit., p. 17.

At the same time, the importance of the private sector to Iranian economic development is appreciated. The profit sharing formula was in no way meant to give laborers managerial control. While the government has not been willing to adopt wage controls, it has served notice to the workers that in the future bonuses will be awarded only for gains in productivity. In the past, employers were required to pay bonuses regardless of their profit situation and efficiency performance. This change in government policy should relax the burdens on private investors.

There continues to be an abiding government concern that the private sector play a larger economic role but within the guidelines and plans established by the government.

THE FIFTH PLAN AND BEYOND

Indications are that not all of the Fifth Plan's targets will be achieved. The initial euphoria of 1973 has given way to the perception that rates of growth exceeding 20 percent are not sustainable without destructive inflation and waste. Oil production and revenues in 1975 and 1976 were below 1974 levels, but it is not clear that capital shortage is Iran's major economic problem although Iran has apparently resorted to the European capital markets recently and there are indications that the government is now strapped for cash. Rather inadequate physical infrastructure, manpower shortages in certain skilled sectors and attendant inflation appear to be more serious impediments to economic development.

If the Fifth Plan's targets were not achieved and some projects will have to be carried over into the Sixth Plan period (1978–83), growth was still impressive and there is now a much more sober assessment of Iran's capabilities. The change in cabinet in 1977 can be viewed in the context of a development plan which went awry and a new conviction that economic management required a somewhat different team headed by a proved, competent and tough administrator. The very change itself implied a warning that waste would be tolerated no longer and marked a victory for those who urged caution, slower rates of economic growth, matching spending with absorptive capacity and extending the "life" of oil reserves.

The oil sector remains crucial to sustained economic growth and Government economic activity. There is today much less optimism regarding Iran's ability to increase production significantly. Earlier official targets called for installed capacity of 8 million barrels a day by the early 1980's. Currently, even with substantial investments in secondary recovery ($4.5 billion in the period 1976–82), oil production is not expected to exceed 6.5 million barrels a day. Moreover, to the extent that domestic consumption increases, Iran may have no more than 5 million barrels a day available for export in the 1980's.[18] With estimated proved reserves of some 60 billion barrels, Iran's reserves-to-production ratio is between 25 to 30 years. It may not be that Iran's revenues will fall catastrophically but more that claims on Government revenues are increasing more rapidly than revenue itself.

The initial step is the emphasis on capturing the value added in downstream petroleum operations. The Shah has repeatedly stated

[18] Financial Times, op cit., p 11.

that oil is to important to be wasted in use as a fuel source. However, Iran's plans for large domestic export refineries have faltered on the unwillingness of Iran's oil customers in Europe and Japan, already suffering from their own surplus refining capacity, to liberalize their tariff regimes in favor of greater product imports.

Petrochemical operations are being expanded and the investment will be substantial; $3.5 billion during the Sixth Plan. Six units are in operation and four others are planned. In 1965, the Government created the National Petrochemical Co. of Iran. There is concern however, that the Iranian petrochemical plans when placed in the context of the petrochemical plans of other Gulf countries will result in overcapacity and depressed prices. In addition, there is a strong possibility that Iran's production costs will be high and petrochemicals exports may require Government subsidies if they are to be internationally competitive.

There is also a much more sobering estimate of natural gas potential. Iran may have the world's second largest gas reserves, after the Soviet Union. However, much of this gas will be utilized domestically and huge quantities may be used in the oil industry's secondary recovery program. Gas exports will increase as current projects become operational in the 1980's [19] but Iran has already announced that it will not contract any additional gas sales. Substantial improvements in gas export earnings may, therefore, depend on increased world natural gas prices and a breakthrough in LNG and gas transportation technology.

In the longer term the idea is to transform the economy into an industrial one before the oil revenues begin to decline and to substitute exports of other goods for declining oil exports. As far as Government-owned industry is concerned Iran hopes to export copper and steel. (Iran also has sizable reserves of coal, iron ore, zinc, lead, and chromite which will be exploited for domestic use.)

Again the problem seems less one of the "oil running out" and more that the claims on Government revenue are increasing rapidly. Having decided to embark on ambitious social welfare schemes, these are not easy to cut back; one gets locked into these expenditures because of the expectations they generate. In addition, the civilian bureaucracy continues to provide employment of the last resort for university-trained individuals who typically react badly to unemployment; 65 percent of the current account budget goes to wages. Military expenditures have been cut back by $2.3 billion in the 1977–78 budget, but even here the regime may be cautious of going too far—at least, in part because of the real security threats perceived by the regime and in part, because of an unwillingness to unsettle the military. Military expenditures account for 24 percent of the current budget. And the price of courting the urban classes is food and other subsidies; in 1976–77 food subsidies cost the Government $1.2 billion, equivalent to 9 percent of current account expenditures.[20]

Iran's development to date has been relatively painless. There was no need to squeeze the agriculture sector for investment funds. Business and individuals were not burdened with heavy taxes; oil revenues

---

[19] A pipeline is being built to service the 1975 Iranian-U.S.S.R. "switch deal" whereby Iran will supply gas to Soviet consuming centers with the Soviets, in turn, supplying nearly equivalent quantities of gas to Western Europe. LNG projects are also in the works.
[20] Financial Times Survey, op. cit., p. 11.

financed Government activities and investment. Something could be done for everyone; oil provided the means and the difficult task of setting priorities was not as urgent as it can be in other countries.

However, with the continued development of the economy and society conflicts of interest begin to appear. For example the need to provide adequate incentives to farmers conflicts with the desire to keep agricultural prices low for consumers. Rapidly rising labor costs unaccompanied by increasing labor productivity, conflict with the desire to make Iranian goods internationally competitive. Rising per capita incomes result in increased demands for consumer goods and imports while the Government is reluctant to crack down through taxation. If increasing amounts of Government expenditures are already committed, the painless situation may no longer prevail and the politics of development will emerge. It may become increasingly difficult to do everything at once and to everyone's satisfaction.

In part the answer lies with the private sector. The relationship with the Government is one of mutual need and mutual ambivalence. The Government is often arbitrary in the application of policies and bureaucratic regulations change daily. Uncertainty is not conducive to increased private sector activity.

Price controls, increasing labor costs, share participation and profit sharing have discouraged private domestic and foreign investors. Foreign investors are also discouraged by restrictions on the amount of equity they can hold in an enterprise. More recently, the Government appears to have become more lenient regarding foreign equity participation and in other ways has indicated the need to encourage private foreign and domestic investment.

Reform of the civilian bureaucracy might also help and the current Government policy of decentralization suggests a recognition of the problem of the bureaucracy. It is an enormous task to push the bureaucratic machinery weighed down by a system which rewards following directions rather than individual responsibility and innovation. There are still too few capable people and they are young and stretched to capacity.

In addition, there are several simultaneous balancing acts which must be maintained in equilibrium. Can the balance between social discipline and the need to mobilize people for the development effort be maintained? The three reform policies discussed in this chapter were designed to mobilize people for the development effort within the guidelines established by the Government. The entire nation is to be positively engaged in the transformation of Iran.

The balance between mobilization and participation is weighted in favor of the former: the question is, are they separable? The view is that people are not adequately educated or prepared to define the goals or the means. And Iran cannot afford the luxury of endless debate, inaction, lack of direction and lack of national (as opposed to regional and functional) leadership which seems to have afflicted the West in recent years and the divisiveness characteristic of other developing countries.

To stress the enormity of Iran's economic development, diversification and industrialization efforts is not to minimize the enormous achievements already accomplished. The slowdown in economic activity preceded the decline in oil revenue; there is a need for: (1) a period of consolidation of gains and a reassessment of capabilities; and (2) a more realistic rate of economic growth minimizing dislocations, distortions and waste. In addition, the slowdown may not be unwelcome in that it extends the period of time during which oil revenues will be substantial. The difficulties which lie ahead must be set against the fact that the Government does recognize the problems, that an increasingly competent group of planners are addressing them and that there is a sense of urgency impelling the effort.

It is an intensity which brooks no opposition, but the perceived stakes are high (internationally and domestically) and it is impossible to know how much time is available. When will oil revenues begin to decline? Can alternatives to oil income and export earnings be found before that date? Will new political forces emerge to provide support for the regime quickly enough to replace more traditional sources of political support which may be eroded in the development process? Can national integration and consensus be achieved before demands for political participation (in the Western sense) develop?

There have been very real advances in standards of living and social welfare. It may be that the regime supports social welfare objectives only to gain popular support or only to preempt potential sources of opposition or only to provide a defense against subversion or only to give people a stake in the system or only to expand the size of the domestic market. But motivation should not detract from the accomplishments.

The tasks ahead will not be easier in spite of past gains. And it is not certain that Iran today and perhaps not for another decade or more, is capable of high rates of economic growth without continued high levels of oil income.

IMPLICATIONS

OIL POLICY

The continued importance of oil revenues to domestic economic, social, and political developments will be reflected in Iran's oil policy. Iran recognizes its interest in the continuous flow of oil to markets. Iranians are quick to point out that Iran has never participated in an oil embargo against the West and Japan and would find it extremely difficult to do so for any extended period of time except in the unlikely event that the issue prompting the embargo so united all OPEC producers that the oil-rich members would compensate Iran for refraining to sell.

Iranians emphasize their past willingness to allow their oil to be used in ways which partially offset the effects of an Arab oil embargo. Moreover, it was Iran's willingness to supply Israel with oil that permitted the Israelis to return the Sinai fields to Egypt. While Iran emphasizes the degree to which it has cooperated with the consuming nations, this is balanced against an Iranian desire to maintain OPEC as an effective organization.

In fact Iran has been in the forefront of those OPEC members seeking to extend the role of the organization. It was under Iran's prodding that OPEC has established a mechanism for exchanging information on petrochemical developments and it is possible that Iran will encourage discussions of gas developments within the OPEC framework. In addition, by giving the OPEC organization a greater role the influence of individual states—Saudi Arabia—would be reduced within the context of that group of OPEC countries with high revenue needs and low proved reserve estimates—Iran, Venezuela, Indonesia, Nigeria, and Algeria.

Within OPEC, Iran has been one of those producing nations arguing for price increases higher than the Saudis have been willing to accept. The real revenue needs of the country and now the likelihood that production will not increase as was once anticipated puts Iran among those nations which seek to maximize revenue from each barrel of oil produced. The prospects for extending the period during which oil production will sustain domestic development and the slowdown in economic activity post-1975 argues in favor of lower production levels and higher prices, the latter objective often putting Iran at odds with Saudi Arabia (witness the 1976 Doha meeting and the subsequent price split).

Iran also has argued strenuously for indexation of oil export prices to the rate of inflation in the industrialized countries. Iran has noted President Carter's acceptance of indexation with regard to domestic oil prices. The Shah also has argued that the price of oil should be linked to the price of alternative energy sources, i.e., above current oil prices. More recently Iran has proposed the linking of oil prices to the rate of inflation in the exports of the industrialized countries (as opposed to the overall inflation rate prevailing in the developed countries).[21]

The price and indexation issues have been contentious ones within OPEC but this may be less the case in the future. Now Iran apparently is counting on the emergence of a tight oil demand/supply situation in the early 1980's. With a relatively weak current oil market Iran apparently is willing to wait for the tight demand/supply situation when prices will rise naturally and when even expansions in Saudi production may not be sufficient to exert downward pressure on prices.

In line with Iranian efforts to maximize the national benefits of oil exploitation, Iran will: (1) promote the expansion and development of the National Iranian Oil Co. (NIOC); (2) renew efforts to export refined products; and (3) attempt to gain experience in all phases of the oil industry through foreign investment—BP joint tanker company, joint exploration with BP in the North Sea, refining projects in India, South Korea, and South Africa and the purchase of 700,000 shares in BP.

In essence while Iran has been cooperative vis-a-vis consuming nations, oil policy will be shaped by a commitment to the maintenance of OPEC solidarity and concern for consumers will not alter Iran's commitment to extracting the maximum benefits from the exploitation of oil, a depletable resource.

Finally, given the importance of oil revenues, there is a felt need to husband oil and gas reserves for export which results in an emphasis on nuclear energy as a domestic energy source.

OTHER IMPLICATIONS

The description of Iran is one of a developing country and, therefore, it should not be surprising to see Iran aligned with other LDC's and against the developed countries on a number of important issues.

---

[21] See Reza Fallah and Fereidun Fesharaki in the "OPEC Review," forthcoming.

Iran was initially an enthusiastic supporter of the Conference on International Economic Cooperation (CIEC). However, as the oil revenues became stretched and the demands from other LDC's for ever-increasing quantities of aid became more insistent, some of Iran's enthusiasm dissipated. Iranian foreign aid will be increasingly geared to Iranian political objectives.

Given Iran's industrialization goals, Iran will find itself aligned with the LDC's in pushing for trade liberalization in industrialized countries within the General Agreement on Tariffs and Trade (GATT) negotiations and on a bilateral basis. Iran has been active in seeking a special position in EC trade (after a 1962 nonpreferential trade agreement was terminated in 1972). Iranian efforts to date to obtain access to European markets for Iranian petroleum product exports have not had any success, as already noted. Moreover, Iran is concerned that the country not be excluded from what appears to be the development of trading blocs (that is, the EC-Arab dialog is watched with uneasiness).

Iran shares with other LDC's a conviction that technology transfers from the industrialized countries to the LDC's should be accelerated and geared to the needs of the recipient country.

Iran is disappointed in the level of foreign investment in Iran and is currently trying to work out greater incentives for foreign investors. There is little comprehension as to the objections of the developed countries with regard to Iranian foreign investment in their industries. As Iran seeks training opportunities and eventually income via outward foreign direct investment, hostility to that investment (and various other policies of the developed countries) is viewed as a purposeful unwillingness on the part of the industrialized countries to assist Iranian development.

In short, it should not be surprising that Iran sometimes will find itself in the "south" camp of the "north-south" dialogs while the industrialization effort has the immediate effect of increasing Iran's involvement with the industrialized "north". Industrialization requires continued access to Western technology, management services, and inputs of raw materials and intermediate goods.

Even in the case of oil, Iran still requires the services of the Oil Services Co. to manage the fields, transport facilities and the secondary recovery effort. Relations with the Oil Services Co. are good in spite of the fact that the company is not: (1) lifting oil in the quantities agreed in the 1973 sales and purchase agreement; (2) investing the sums specified in the agreement; and (3) planning to continue to take oil products from the government-owned Abadan refinery. A new agreement between NIOC and the Oil Services Co. will probably follow completion of a Saudi-Aramco settlement.

Finally, the emphasis on industrialization has resulted also in a great deal of diplomatic activity designed to foster better regional political relations and regional cooperation. The need to expand non-oil exports has impelled Iran in this direction. Iran's regional policy is, in part, predicated on Iran's future mercantile needs.[22]

---

[22] R. M. Burrell, "Iranian Foreign Policy: Strategic Location, Economic Ambition and Dynastic Determination," *Journal of International Affairs*, Vol. 29, No. 2, 1975.

IV. THE POLITICAL SYSTEM

INTRODUCTION

Given Iran's strategic location, its importance to the continued flow of oil in world trade and its role as oil supplier to U.S. allies in Western Europe and Japan, the United States cannot be indifferent to political developments and changes which may have a bearing on: (1) Iranian oil policy; (2) the continued availability of Iranian and Gulf oil; and (3) the United States-Iranian relationship. For example, will political change imply a change in Iran's oil policy?
Are there circumstances under which the government would find it politically inopportune to be linked with the United States or the West? Is the political system conducive to the achievement of the country's economic goals? The importance of these and other questions necessitates an analysis of Iran's political past, present, and future.

POLITICAL DEVELOPMENT

Much of Iran's political development in this century was associated with a nationalism which had its essential basis in antiforeign feeling. In terms of Iran's internal development it remains a chord to be struck by the government or opposition forces and it must be taken into account by any Iranian regime. Moreover, it is not unlikely that this antiforeign component of Iranian nationalism will influence Iran's external relations, including United States-Iranian relations.

As already noted the constitutionalist movement of 1906–7 arose from dissatisfaction with the poor and arbitrary government administration and economic and political difficulties which were attributed to foreign intervention. Opposition to the economic concessions being granted to foreigners and the conviction that the regime was "selling" Iran to foreigners also inspired the constitutionalists. It is ironic then that it was foreign (British) intervention in support of the constitutionalists which permitted them to successfully oppose the Shah (who was supported by the Russians).

The constitutional experiment was interrupted by the outbreak of World War I, the occupation of the country by the British and the Russians, fighting between these two and the Ottomans on Iranian territory and German incitement among the tribes. With the end of the war, the British attempted to force Iranian acceptance of a treaty that would have reduced Iran to a British protectorate, the Soviets supported secessionist movements in the north and the tribes were in open rebellion against the authority of the central government.

It was under these circumstances that civilian and military nationalists under the leadership of Sayid Zia ed-Din Taba-Tabai and Reza Khan, respectively, joined forces in a coup d'etat unseating the government in 1921. In 1925, the Majlis deposed the Qajar dynasty and named Reza Khan the new monarch and founder of the Pahlavi dynasty.

Reza Shah's first acts involved freeing the country from Russian and British influence. The military, which until this point had consisted of the Russian-organized Persian Cossack Brigade, the British-officered South Persian Rifles and the Swedish-trained gendarmarie was unified and strengthened. Agreement with the Soviet Union resulted in reduced Soviet support for the northern secessionists who were then defeated by the Iranian army. The proposed British treaty was rejected.

The capitulations were abolished in 1927. The responsibility for issuing Persian bank notes was transferred from the British to a Persian national bank. The oil agreement with the Anglo-Persian Oil Company (later Anglo-Iranian, currently British Petroleum) was amended in Iran's favor in 1933. Closer ties were established with Germany to offset British and Russian influence. Apparently none of these acts was seen to be inconsistent with the use of foreign advisors in the modernization programs undertaken during Reza Shah's rule.

However, whatever was accomplished came to a complete halt when with the outbreak of World War II Iran was occupied again. The Shah abdicated in favor of his 21-year-old son, Mohammed Reza Shah Pahlavi, the current ruler.

During the war, the allies released the khans from Tehran where they had been "invited" to reside by Reza Shah and they again assumed control of their tribes. The Communists, imprisoned under Reza Shah's regime, were released. Political parties were allowed to organize and the Russians supported the Tudeh Party, while the British supported the conservative National Will Party. All the political forces decimated or forced underground by Reza Shah re-emerged with vigor. The economy was shattered.

When the war was over and the foreign forces finally evacuated, Iran looked very similar to post-World War I Iran, with the added complication that there was to be a protracted struggle for power between the young Shah and the resuscitated Majlis. The end of the war and the occupation witnessed the emergence of a political free-for-all in Iran.

In 1947, nationalists, religious groups, students, bazaaris, socialists and Communists had coalesced in the National Front headed by Muhammed Musaddiq. Capitalizing on the antiforeign sentiment rampant in post-war Iran and the chronic economic distress then prevailing, the nationalists seized the oil issue to gain popular support and to enhance their position vis-a-vis the Shah. The foreign oil company refused to give Iran a greater share of the benefits to be derived from the exploitation of Iran's only (at the time) important natural resource and the effect was explosive.

In 1951, the Majlis voted to nationalize the assets of the Anglo-Iranian Oil Co. The move was immensely popular and shifted the balance of political power in favor of the nationalists in the Majlis and against the Shah. The nationalization was also economically devastating. With oil exports effectively embargoed by the major oil companies, the economy continued to deteriorate.

The nationalization remained popular, and when Musaddiq did eventually fall it was on the real political issue at stake; that is, the relative power of the Shah and the Majlis. When Musaddiq began assuming dictatorial powers, dispensing with the Majlis and seeking control of the military, some of his followers became disenchanted and rallied, with some of the military, to the Shah.

In addition, the inability to reach an oil agreement in spite of numerous American attempts to reconcile the two sides, convinced the United States that a continuation of the crisis could result only in a Communist takeover of the government. In 1953, units of the Iranian army staged a coup d'etat, apparently with American assistance, deposing Musaddiq and restoring the Shah to power.

In 1906–07, 1921 and 1951–54, political developments were related to the nationalistic reaction against foreign intervention in Iranian affairs. Deeper issues of political power were at stake but the issue used to generate popular support was the antiforeign dimensions of Iranian nationalism. Iran could accept paid foreign advisors when it was deemed expedient and when advice was requested but antiforeignism hit a responsive chord within Iranian society.

Two factors deserve to be stressed. First, in spite of its negative economic consequences, the oil nationalization and the Musaddiq period are still viewed by Iranians as a period of national triumph and a source of national pride. The oil nationalization and antiforeignism were popular; the Shah says he supported the nationalization measure and he could not say or do otherwise. Nationalization was never repudiated although at this time its effects were more cosmetic than real.

Second, whatever the American role in restoring the Shah to power, the reality of the role is assumed. Continuing U.S. military aid was viewed as the means by which the Shah built the military and the secret police, and these in turn are viewed by some as the principal means by which the Shah maintains himself in power.

The Shah and the Monarchy

The conclusion is inescapable that the Iranian political system depends fundamentally for its direction, content and perhaps continuity on a single individual and a small coterie of lieutenants. Under these circumstances, the Shah's visions for Iran's future and his political strength will determine the shape of Iran's domestic and international political, economic, social and military developments.

Westerners are generally uncomfortable with systems in which the presence or absence of a single individual can be so very consequential. In terms of Iran, this system reflects thousands of years of historical experience as well as the preference of the incumbent. The advent of a modern military and security establishment, improved transportation and communications facilities and greater resources at the disposal of the government for distribution simply make the system more efficient and more pervasive. Yet it is inescapable that there is a fragility in a system so dependent on one individual.

The Shah apparently believes in the necessity for this type of centralized rule to induce rapid economic change. When the landlords enjoyed great influence and peasants voted as they were told, the argument runs, governments were dominated by conservative interests opposed to change. Apparently the problem is resolved in that peasants may still vote as they are told but now the government does the telling and candidates are subject to government approval.

The monarchical, tutelary type of rule is therefore, believed to be most consistent with Iran's historical experience, best suited to Iran's social conditions and most appropriate to the achievement of Iran's development goals. Parliamentary systems which appear to be indecisive, incapable of positive action and stymied by the exercise of those very freedoms they are committed to uphold are not considered an appropriate model for Iran. Iran's development goals are set, there is little room or tolerance for dissent and debate is limited to, at the very most, appropriate means of achieving those goals.

Philosophically the regime's position is apparently that political change is to be introduced gradually and certainly not "prematurely". The key words are discipline, responsibility and timing. Until the lessons of social responsibility and responsibility to Iran's future are learned, until the population is literate and capable of "constructive" views, until people have learned and accepted what Iran is to be and their role in achieving it, the time for political change will not have arrived.

A great deal of economic and social change is a precondition for political change. When a national consensus consistent with the Shah's vision for Iran has been achieved and when economic and social developments have brought every one into the fold some sort of unspecified political change will be either unnecessary or, alternatively, possible and orderly.

Groups will then emerge based on issues and interests derived from the increasing complexity of the society, not on the ideological fervor and personalism which characterized past political development. Only then can political development be constructive.

All of this may have validity but the list of preconditions is long and even when fulfilled the definition of acceptable political change probably does not include any diminishment of the monarchical prerogatives. The danger is that the Shah will never accept that these conditions have materialized, or will never allow them to materialize, because they are not consistent with the preponderant role he believes he must have in order to lead the transformation of Iran into a modern industrial nation.

Most Iranians do not speak of political development. But the question remains, after people become "responsible" what is it that they are responsible for? Will a responsible populace participate in political power? How can the man with the determination to mold Iran according to his views share power? There is probably some agreement that the system requires centralized direction; we are not speaking of participatory democracy but rather of who will do the directing.

For those who will speculate there is only frustration and cynicism regarding the regime's intentions and its ability to countenance political change. The system depends on an economic determinism which states that with economic progress all human needs are satisfied; history has suggested the reverse—when economic needs are approximated political and ideological goals emerge.

And if for the Shah the only choices he can visualize are the current regime or a radical regime, he may find himself in the midst of a self-fulfilling prophecy.

Goals

In the immediate future the power and visions of the ruling Shah are critical. In addition the goals are apparently widely-agreed. With the conviction that political developments remain for some time in the future, Iran's goals are stated largely in economic terms. What is interesting in terms of the question of continued access to Iranian oil is that they link Iran firmly to the West at the same time that there is a resentment of the West and the antiforeign sentiment previously described.

The Shah has repeatedly stated that his essential goal is for Iran to assume a place of equality with the world's major industrial powers. Iran is to reach the living standards currently prevailing in the European countries in the next 10 to 15 years. It is irrelevant that the target date extends farther into the future; once the goal was to be achieved in 1985, now the date is 1990. The direction is clear.

What seems to Westerners as bravado and pretentiousness is animated by a sense of urgency and nationalism borne of the conviction that the humiliations of the past must not be repeated. There is simultaneously a desire to emulate the West and a resentment of past treatment at the hands of the industrialized countries (including the Soviet Union).

While there is a recognition that Western means and institutions may not function as expected in a non-Western environment, there is much less critical examination of the goals and these remain very largely associated with the West: Industrialization, social welfare, military strength. In the Iranian context modernization is tantamount to Westernization.

Historically this has been partially reflected in Iran's reliance on Western advisors from various countries in various functions. This was true under the Qajars and continued under Reza Shah's regime.

The models Iranians point to are in the United States, Western Europe and Japan. The United States is attractive because of its economic strength and assumed technical superiority. The Germans are attractive for essentially the same reasons. The Japanese hold a special attraction because of their success in the economic sphere while apparently retaining that which is uniquely Japanese in culture and values.

For Iran too, there is concern to retain that which is uniquely Persian. The goal is to find some optimal amalgamation of what is best in Iran with what is best in the West. There is the sense that Iran should be able to benefit from the developmental experiences of the industrialized countries (East and West) and other less developed countries to find what may be applicable to Iran and to avoid the pitfalls associated with developments elsewhere; that is, alienation, polarization, and political instability. By picking and choosing selectively, the hope is to design a new and creative synthesis that is superior to developments in either Iran or the West separately.

There may be ambivalence toward the West and resentment as to its dealings with Iran but the goals link Iran to the industrialized countries in the West and Japan—an important consideration in Iran's oil policy and the United States-Iranian relationship.

Functioning of the System

Given the political views of the Shah and his goals for Iran, the further question relates to the ability of this political system to achieve its goals. If the system is not conducive to goal achievement, the negative implications for economic development and political stability could be substantial.

Not all the failings of the system relate to the Shah's influence. But the nature of the Shah's rule, its secrecy, arbitrariness, and the insecurity it generates in those people responsible for development has done nothing to alleviate the system's shortcomings.

Moreover, if the system is not conducive to plan fulfillment, the frustration engendered may find release in a foreign scapegoat for foreign adventures.

Political and Social Forces

The military and internal security forces represent an essential element of support for the regime. The Shah takes a personal interest in the military, involving himself in weapons acquisition, military training, and promotions to the upper levels of the officer corps. The military is supplied with the latest weaponry and is generally treated as a privileged group.

The Shah also keeps them on a tight rein. The aim is to keep the military content, occupied and incapable of political action against the regime. The need to keep the military satisfied and the element of prestige must be factored into any assessment of Iranian arms purchases.

Interestingly the Shah's father also staked a great deal of Iran's national pride on the military. It collapsed when confronted with the British and Russian invasion in 1941 and the military lost a great deal of popular support. The military is not necessarily popular.

There are three intelligence services. The most widely known is SAVAK which is alleged to have been formed and organized with the assistance of the U.S. Central Intelligence Agency and later, Israeli intelligence forces may have assisted also. Contacts between the CIA and SAVAK are believed to continue. Opponents of the regime who see that the Shah's rule depends on the strength of the military and security forces also see that it was (and to some extent, still is), American assistance which promoted their growth and development. The presumed American support for the Shah should not be discounted: it may have considerable deterrent value against those seeking change and engender considerable resentment as well.

Apart from the military basis of support is the small group of officials who occupy the top administrative posts and the Council of Ministers. These are the "aristocrats" of the Iranian system with personal, ideological, or business ties to the Shah, the Pahlavi family or Reza Shah; they are members of the important families whose influence often extends back as far as Qajar days.

Once the Shah embarked on his economic plans, this group, the only one having a modern education at that time, became essential. The group is small and it has changed little over the years. Even the Cabinet appointed in the summer of 1977 contains a majority of old faces. In part, this stability in personnel relates to the very real shortage of skilled and competent administrators. In part, there are simply few other, private opportunities and in part, longevity in office relates to the fact that trust does not come easily to the regime. They serve at the Shah's discretion and they owe their positions to him.

Recent efforts focus on bringing newly-emerging groups into the system in a constructive way. The process of cooperation through economic incentives has been described. In addition as the government assumes increasing functions, segments of the population become increasingly dependent on it, that is, the middle class depends on government jobs, farmers depend on the government for credit and seed, et cetera.

At the same time that their dependence increases, their expectations of what government is responsible for providing increases as well. As some of the old bases of acquiescence and support fall away (religion), the newer bases of loyalty (economic advance and government services), have not reached large parts of the population. The peasants remain politically inert. Government efforts to broaden the base of political support continue.

The greatest efforts have been made to win the educated, urban upper and middle classes and the professionals. These are the technocrats on whom so very much of Iran's future achievements will rest. The greatest number of them are located at all levels of the civilian bureaucracy. And an increasing number of them come from lower and middle class backgrounds.

If in one sense it is true that Iran has not had a popular revolution à la the French model, it is also true that there has been a great deal of change in the relative position of various societal groups. The first several Majlis—up until the early 1960's—were dominated by landlords. In the 1960's, the upper middle classes and the professionals accounted for 69 percent of the seats in the Majlis.

By 1975, the Majlis was dominated by medium-sized farmers, teachers, professionals, middle-ranking bureaucrats, some businessmen and a few peasants. Eighty percent of the people elected to the Majlis were new to Parliament. In part, the high rate of turnover may guarantee that the Majlis will be inexperienced and docile.

And yet there has been increasing criticism of the regime in the Majlis and the new members may be less amenable to direction than the rich and powerful members of the now-defunct Iran Novin Party. The Majlis, historically, has been willing to challenge the Shah in spite of his extensive powers over the selection of candidates, his ability to dissolve Parliament and his selection of 50 percent of the members of the more conservative, upper house. Further challenges from this source either in terms of policy or the extent of the Shah's prerogatives cannot be ruled out and it may be increasingly difficult to simply dissolve the Majlis as the Shah did in the 1960's.

The silent opposition and malaise of many of the same forces which supported the National Front might make it difficult to merely dissolve the Majlis. The Front was still active in the 1960's. It is an amorphous coalition consisting of people who are generally uneasy about the regime, often for varying reasons. In the past these isolated forces under the right kind of leadership, did prove to be mobilizable. And it is this group and the bureaucratic, technocratic middle class that the Shah must take into account.

But this may remain for some time opposition within permissible bounds. For those who refuse to be co-opted the regime is not necessarily lenient. The greater effort is to bring people into the establishment; even when reducing the position or power of a particular individual he may be left enough to give him a stake in the system. If he still refuses to be co-opted possible government action includes exile, prison and, in the last resort, execution.

If there is an organized opposition it is difficult to judge its extent because SAVAK operations force opposition activities into secret and underground groups. The Tudeh surfaced again in the 1951–54 crisis and again in the 1960's, having infiltrated segments of the military. A pro-Soviet faction operates out of East Germany and a pro-Peking faction exists.

The Freedom Movement of Iran, which demands a republican form of government, is an offshoot of the National Front. Apparently it is divided between a left-wing and a religious faction. The Shah attributes the sporadic acts of urban terrorism to a coalition of forces which he labels Islamic-Marxist. By-and-large the extremist groups appear to be no more than a nuisance and an embarrassment to the regime.

The pressures for change exist and it may be the Shah's attitude which determines whether change can be orderly. There is little reason to be sanguine.

Political Dynamics

Every society co-opts individuals who might otherwise oppose it and does so with a measure of success (in the West it is called social mobility) Iran may be no exception. The problem with co-optation in Iran, however, may be that while it silences people it may not necessarily engage them in a positive way, perhaps permitting others to do so. Also successful co-optation requires time and while it can and does go some way toward assuring popular acquiescence it does not resolve all the problems of effective and popular government.

There is a real possibility that the internal dynamics of the system are such that it will be extremely difficult to achieve the Government's goals. The fundamental principle of Iranian politics appears to be that the emergence of alternative or additional independent sources of power will not be tolerated with a number of negative consequences for the effective functioning of the system.

First, the prohibitions against the development of autonomous centers of power inhibits political institutionalization. There is no distinct group of professional politicians to lend continuity and expertise to the system. A host of government-supported political parties have come and gone with no apparent sense of loss. The Majlis does not now function to control the Government.

In terms of the bureaucratic institution, because a job well done is just as likely to result in demotion as promotion, there is little incentive to accept responsibility or to be innovative. The inability to countenance individual sources of influence also makes the system arbitrary, dependent on the Shah and personalism and generates insecurity and caution in those who quite literally may be here today and gone tomorrow. In addition, groups and individuals may be set against each other or given identical functions to check the influence of both.

The system depends on balance, rivalry and tension which may be highly effective in preventing the emergence of autonomous power centers but inconsistent with efficiency and effectiveness. The Shah continues the lack of institutionalization which resulted in chaos when his father abdicated.

ALTERNATIVE REGIMES AND IMPLICATIONS

Any alternative regime would face a complex balance of factors. The Soviet threat, the continued need for Western and Japanese technical assistance, trade and oil markets and perhaps the Western education and orientation of the elite mitigate against anything but rhetorical antiforeignism.

At the same time, the United States need to defend Iran almost regardless of internal political developments and the very real need of Europe and Japan for Iranian oil give Iran some freedom of maneuver; particularly vis-a-vis the United States.

But to the extent that Iran's goals do not change, and there appears to be agreement on ends, Iran will depend on oil revenues. Iran will have to export oil and the markets will continue to be in Western Europe and Japan. United States-Iranian relations may some times be strained but Iranian-Western ties are essential to Iran's development.

However, the further question of the destination of oil imports could be affected if the Soviets or East Europeans actually require substantial oil imports. Pressure on Iran in the north or from Iraq or Afghanistan—with Soviet prodding—could be used to compel Iran to divert some oil exports to the Eastern bloc. But even then Iran will require hard currency earnings and these will require oil exports to the West.

A government more heavily influenced by religion—which seems unlikely given the increasing secularization of the society—might find Iran alined with its coreligionists in the Arab countries, perhaps including Iranian participation in a future oil embargo.

In general foreign intervention has been a sensitive issue in Iran. Foreigners have always been used as sources of advice, technology, goods and capital. Perhaps then not too much stock should be placed on the amount of influence associated with this foreign role.

Iranians themselves are eager to continue to diversify their contacts with the West and Japan so as to avoid the appearance of undue dependence on any of them. From a U.S. perspective there is nothing objectionable in this policy. Relations with the Shah that are too close or too exclusive might damage his domestic position as well as the capacity of the United States to deal with successor regimes. The requirement is for a sensitive management of United States-Iranian relations.

PART V

I. IMPLICATIONS FOR THE UNITED STATES

1. The United States has diverse, multiple and growing ties with Iran and Saudi Arabia. However, in terms of oil trade, Western Europe and Japan are larger markets for Saudi and Iranian oil than is the United States. Western Europe and Japan are more dependent on these sources of oil imports than is the United States. The United States received only 8 percent of its total oil consumption from Saudi Arabia and less than 2 percent from Iran in 1976.

In part, the U.S. interest in the Gulf is derived from the greater dependence of U.S. allies on these sources of oil imports and serves the collective security interest of the Western and Japanese alliance. The United States could not remain unaffected by developments which reduced the security and adequacy of supply to U.S. allies. Given the importance of the resources of Iran and Saudi Arabia a successful move by a third power which interrupts the flow of oil would be a very major threat to the industrialized countries of the West and Japan.

Moreover, to the extent that U.S. oil import demand increases much of that demand may have to be met from Gulf production. U.S. imports from Saudi Arabia increased from 440,000 barrels per day in 1974 to 1,200,000 in 1976; U.S. imports of crude oil from the United Arab Emirates increased from 69,000 barrels per day in 1974 to 255,000 barrels per day in 1976.

The U.S. interest in the Gulf is thus a reflection both of the vital interests of allies and of its own growing dependence upon Middle East oil. It will remain so for as long as oil imports are required. A U.S. commitment to the defense of the oil resources of the Gulf and to political stability in the region must constitute one of the most vital and enduring interests of the United States.

2. The United States has a direct interest in a defensible and politically stable Iran. That nation continues to serve as a deterrent against Soviet adventurism in the region; moreover a strong and stable Iran also serves as a deterrent against radical groups in the Gulf.

3. The United States has a crucial interest in maintaining access to the vital oil reserves of Saudi Arabia. The United States has a complementary interest in the political stability of the kingdom and its pursuit of oil policies which are fundamental to the adequacy and continuity of supply to the world's importing nations.

4. The U.S. stake in Iran and Saudi Arabia is unprecedented and reflects geostrategic and energy interests of great magnitude. Yet the past record of mistrust between these two Middle East states, and the probability that Iran's present dependence upon oil revenue for its development will raise acute questions as to how it will cope with its economic, social and military expenditures, as compared to a Saudi

Arabia, possessed of staggering amounts of oil and a revenue far beyond its needs are nearly certain to heighten tension between them. The United States will have to be exceptionally alert to possible confrontations between these two kingdoms in which the evident mutual interests of both parties may be obscured at great risk to other nations in the Gulf and to the world at large.

5. It is evident that the U.S. presence in the Gulf does contribute to security of supply; moreover, it is equally clear that no other nation of the non-Communist world can substitute now or for the foreseeable future for the United States. The "special relationship" which the United States has forged with Iran and Saudi Arabia has different origins but these do not make for contradictory policies and programs. In all likelihood, assuming no serious increase in tension between Iran and Saudi Arabia, the U.S. relationships are reinforcing.

6. The prospect, nevertheless, is not so much for political stability in the region, as in political and social change as economic development occurs. Change need not be abrupt and adverse to United States, European, and Japanese interests. But in a region as volatile as the Gulf there is a greater probability of revolutionary change than of political and social evolution. The question must be asked as to the extent to which change in Iran and Saudi Arabia may affect the continuity and adequacy of oil supply, and the defense of the region against Soviet encroachment.

In the case of Iran, a change in regime is thought unlikely to affect the flow of oil. The revenue needs of any Iranian Government will be such as nearly to compel it to produce at highest possible rates; in the case of Saudi Arabia, a change in regime (or in the policies of the present leadership) could result in a drastic reduction in the volume of oil entering world trade such as to eliminate the present surplus altogether and/or allow for another sudden and drastic increase in price.

It is not likely, however, that a change in regime in either Iran or Saudi Arabia would result in lasting opportunities for Soviet encroachment on the oil reserves of the region. As is pointed out in this report, there is a history of opposition to Russian efforts to extend control or even influence in the area, an opposition which comes close to being a "permanent factor" in Middle East politics.

7. Nevertheless, while there are a multiplicity of longstanding issues between the peoples of the region, stress must still be placed most heavily on the impact no progress on the Arab-Israeli dispute could have on oil supply. Despite the other interests the Iranians and Saudis have in their U.S. link, the pressures on each, but especially upon Saudi Arabia to employ the oil weapon could be acute; we are warned of this repeatedly. Saudi Arabia cannot remain isolated from the events which still count so heavily in the political interests and pressures of the Middle East.

8. We have said there is presently no substitute for the U.S. presence in Middle East oil, primarily to help assure security of supply to allies and secondarily to help assure that its own import needs are met. Yet it would seem only prudent to take steps now to encourage the involvement of European states and Japan in such ways as to diminish the political impact of what may well become too great a U.S. presence

in the national affairs of these two key countries. While Iran has been aware of this need and Saudi Arabia also, the impression persists in Europe and Japan that the present paramount U.S. role in Saudi oil exports could be re-examined by both governments. The far greater importance of Saudi oil to markets in Europe and Japan than to the United States has already been emphasized. If in fact U.S. companies are to have access to 7 MMB/D of Saudi oil, that may well be in the interest of Saudi Arabia, and of the companies, but questions are asked as to the objectives which may be pursued by the U.S. Government in its own "oil diplomacy" through its presumed influence over U.S. oil companies.

9. With regard to the participation of United States companies in Iran's and Saudi Arabia's development, it is greatly in the U.S. interest to see that these are successful and that complaints as to poor performance and overcharging are persuasively answered. It may yet require a degree of U.S. Government involvement and even assumption of responsibility, "vouching" in effect for the American companies, which will be unprecedented for the U.S. Government. Yet the stakes involved in helping Iran and Saudi Arabia are great enough to warrant such a posture, assuming means are found to assist these governments in undertaking projects which are within their reasonable grasp.

○

Printed in the USA
CPSIA information can be obtained
at www.ICGtesting.com
LVHW021544190424
777899LV00002B/173